Curious Encounters

PHANTOM TRAINS, SPOOKY SPOTS,
AND OTHER MYSTERIOUS WONDERS

Loren Coleman

faber and faber
BOSTON • LONDON

Published by Faber and Faber, Inc.
50 Cross Street, Winchester, MA 01890
First printing: August 1985
Second printing: January 1986

Cover design by Deborah Norris
Interior design: Michael Michaud
Composition: WordTech Corporation
Printing and binding: Daamen, Inc.
Cover: New England Book Components

LIBRARY OF CONGRESS CATALOGING IN PUBLICATION DATA
Coleman, Loren.
Curious Encounters

Includes index.
1. United States—Miscellanea. 2. Curiosities and wonders—United States.
I. Title.
E179.C63 1985 001.9'4'0973 85-10132
ISBN 0-571-12542-5 (pbk.)

Printed in the United States of America

To Libbet

Contents

Illustrations

(courtesy of Rod Dyke)

Charles Fort, American intellectual and investigator of the unexplained, at the age of twelve. Many researchers of the unknown have had experiences with unexplained phenomena at an early age. Fort's childhood encounters stimulated his curiosity and propelled him into a life of inquiry.

Acknowledgements

Once again, I would like to thank those 109 individuals, organizations, and publications I mentioned under this heading in *Mysterious America*. All of those folks have helped directly or indirectly in bringing about this book. I agree with Charles Fort, the first modern American to systematically and intellectually investigate the strange and unusual, when he stated, "One measures a circle, beginning anywhere." My investigations and the phenomena merge from one to the next.

Some special Fortean appreciations, however, must be noted. Mark A. Hall continued to be supportive with advice and information and especially gave assistance on the phantom train and mystery spots data. Rod Dyke's and Jerry Clark's input into the chapter on sea machines and sky serpents were helpful. Furthermore, numerous people wrote me for the first time after reading *Mysterious America* and scores passed along worthwhile leads. They range from the reams of alligator-in-the-suburbs items sent by Mark A. Kolodny to the singular kangaroo clipping mailed anonymously from Michigan. I thank all these people for taking the time to route this material my way.

And likewise, a tip of my cap to Apple for producing the Macintosh™, which I used to create this book. I am, as well, indebted to Louise Richardson and Laura Maxwell of Faber and Faber for their fine editing and assembling of this work.

I would also like to take a few extra moments to thank a group of people, non-Forteans all, who have stood by me as I pursued the newest mystery on the horizon. This network has been supportive of my needs to be surrounded with warmth and good cheer when I returned mud-caked from some enigmatic adventure, or merely to be left alone to write "just one more chapter." Foremost among this community, of course, is Libbet. Other important friends and colleagues are Robert, Marian, Enes, Chuck, Dick, Lynn, Tom, Jeanette, John, Judy, Nora, Joel, Mark, Mara, Janet, John, Monique, John, Ted, Mara, Phil, Mary, Joyce, David, Alice, Tom, Helaine, Susan, Beth, Cathy, Janet, Wanda, Connie, Jean, Anne, Carol, and my family: Bill, Susan, Jerry, Mom, and Dad. Probably by now, some of them are even closet Forteans.

My explorations could not have been made without them.

Loren Coleman
April 1985
Maine

INTRODUCTION

It Really is Weird Out There

I shall be accused of having assembled lies, yarns, hoaxes and superstitions. To some degree I think so, myself. To some degree I do not. I offer the data. – *Charles Fort*

The day started off the way it usually did, that Monday 8 October 1984 at the Truckers Inn in Sauk Centre, Minnesota. The smell of fresh coffee, golden toast, and crackling bacon circled in the air over the brown and beige motif of the restaurant. The Truckers Inn had sat at the junction of Highway 71 and Interstate 94 for the last fourteen years, and nothing like what was about to happen had ever occurred there. Oh yah, people locally would talk about the ghost that haunted the old Palmer House in town, but the twenty-four hour truck stop was not your usual idea of a spooky place. Things changed around 8:30 A.M., though, when the truck driving, husband-and-wife team of Robert and Jackie Bair burst into the diner. They needed to use the phone. They were under attack.

Bird-like Aliens from Billings?

The account the couple told seemed like it was straight out of a Rod Serling story, but this story wasn't fictional. They had parked their rig, and they weren't going to move it again. The company was going to have to deal with that problem; they had problems of their own. They were under seige by creatures shaped like birds with human feet and V-shaped heads.

It began somewhere near Billings, Montana, the couple told Sauk

Centre Police Chief George Trierweiler. A bubble-shaped space ship emerged from a dark cloud and began spraying the Bairs' truck with small metal filings. The filings entered the truck's cab and caused a rash on the couple's arms, Robert Bair claimed. Then their truck collided with the space ship, which had crashed beside the road. A peanut-shaped cylinder tumbled out of the craft and creatures, which definitely seemed out-of-this -world, jumped from the cylinder. The "aliens" were eight-inches tall, bird-like, and very intent on continuing to shoot metal filings at the Bairs. The creatures followed the husband-and-wife team from Billings to Sauk Centre.

Trierweiler said that as he talked to the pair in the truck-stop parking lot, they claimed to see bird-like "guards" perched on top of street lights, "workers" in trees, and a red-colored "foreman" nearby. Although he strained to see them, the chief reported he saw nothing. "They went on and on and about drove me nuts," Trierweiler said. "They're definitely afraid of something." He did find evidence of red spots on their arms, but he said it did not look like the truck had been involved in a collision. He also did not see any scratches on the windshield, but discovered some metal filings in the truck's cab. Trierweiler was quick to skeptically observe, "Maybe they had some work done in the truck."

My Talks With Townspeople

Discussing the matter with the folks of Sauk Centre, I found opinion mixed on whether the Blairs should be believed or not. Dorothy Sills, the manager of the Truckers Inn, told me she was really upset, at the time, with the Bairs because after they arrived they tied up the telephones in the place. However, she described them as quiet, neatly dressed, and clean. Sills noted the couple was firm in their belief these creatures were real. At one point, she noted, Robert Bair gestured at the utility poles where he said the creatures were roosting and firing shavings. He yelled, "Here comes another one now!" and ducked. Sills said they ducked a lot: As our interview drew to a close, Dorothy Sills wanted to make certain I knew how sincere the Bairs were. "They definitely believed what they said they saw was real," she told me.

Perhaps no one spent more effort to get to the bottom of the story than *Sauk Centre Herald* reporter Roberta Olson. Olson was one of the few people in town to actually spend some time with the Bairs and, indeed, the only reporter to interview them. She was one of the few people I found who was convinced the Bairs were having some real experiences. The reporter befriended the couple and talked to them for hours about their encounters with the creatures. The Bairs told Olson of the strange matter coming out of the corner of their Sinclair Lewis Motel room walls; of the wings they saw on the back of the creatures; of the metal shavings that were continuing to be thrown their way; of the something-beyond-words that they found on their bed. Roberta Olson was careful and professional in her interviews, but she got the feeling something occult was occurring, and this was way beyond her understanding. As Olson told me, "Something mysterious did happed to those people. You had to see their eyes."

The couple, far from their Selah, Washington home, spent two nights at the motel. They told Olson that the experience continued in their room and writing appeared on Jackie Bair's thigh. And when outside, the bird-men still shot metal filings at the Bairs from the tops of trees and insulator caps. Olson even noted the tips of branches looked blacker the day Robert Bair said they were occupied by the creatures than they did the next day. Something bizarre did seem to be taking place in the little town of Sauk Center.

Meanwhile, back at their trucking homebase in Yakima, Washington, the Scott Davis Transport Company's manager Jim Ketchem was getting tired of answering the phone. Reporters, the Bairs, and local Minnesota authorities had been calling all day. The manager remained convinced the couple were telling the truth. "They are plain, old everyday folks. They're not crazies," Ketchem told the officials. He had to deal with the fact the Bairs were not going to drive their truckful of vegetable fat any further. He sent another driver to Sauk Centre who took the Bairs to Minneapolis, and from there the couple flew back to Washington. After two days of being disbelieved and ridiculed, the Bairs were happy to leave Sauk Centre. "We are accused of being drug addicts and that we're hallucinating," Robert Bair said. "But that's not true."

And then the Bairs disappeared. Reporter Olson and I have both tried to track the couple down, but they are not to be found. Perhaps they needed to vanish and regroup their lives? Or perchance, did the attacks of the birdmen continue?

Vegetarian Aliens? A Folly of Two?

What are we to make of this? Aliens from outer space with an interest in vegetable oil? The ghost of Sauk Centre's Sinclair Lewis in a new guise? Or should we look to the rational explanation that quickly surfaced that these people were insane?

Psychiatric thought would immediately assume these poor folks are suffering from a form of temporary atypical psychoses, a *folie à deux* literally a folly of two. In such a "communicated insanity," a delusion is shared by two or more closely related and associated persons. The dominant person is often labeled schizophrenic, and this individual has elaborate delusions of being controlled by telepathy, X-rays, or spaceships. Often one of the delusional components is Lilliputian hallucinations, that is , perceptions of little people. This of course sounds like the Minnesota case and in some ways focuses the explanation on the individuals. Are we now assured the phenomena can be forgotten?

In the psychology of humans, the labeling of a behavior is often like a nail in a coffin. To have it named to many is to "explain" it. But we must go with caution about such matters. If the folks that said they saw the birdmen from a spaceship had a *folie à deux*, then what does that tell us about the nature of things? Are there aliens? What was the source of the manifestations? Are humans who see the aliens, not seeing aliens? And what is not seeing, and yet not experiencing the image, all about? To place a psychiatric term on an experience does much to reflect the discussion back to the percipient, but it does not answer our questions about why such experiences are occurring now, and in ever-increasing numbers. In some ways, such labeling, be it psychiatric or psychic, does no more to explain the phenomena than to ignore it. Explaining is a form of feeling comfortable with the uncomfortable, and how can we feel at ease with these strange stories?

Out of context, the report of the Bairs appears bizarre and unreal. Perhaps it is; perhaps not. All over the world, meetings between things totally unacceptable to scientists and skeptics are intruding their way into the lives of common, ordinary folk.

Reeves and the Walking Trees

The Sauk Centre encounter is a strange story indeed, but no stranger than the report of sixteen-year-old Kathy Reeves of Newport, Oregon. In April 1966, she said she saw three tiny tree stumps walking across a meadow near her home. And she noted they were orange, blue, white, yellow, and "watermelon"-colored. Soon all hell broke loose around there: UFOs were sighted; Newport residents started talking about how nearby Pioneer Mountain had always been weird; a local couple told officials they had seen a group of staring cyclops; and the Reeves family, who actually lived on the side of Pioneer Mountain, started experiencing waves of poltergeist activity. Objects in their houses danced about and globes of bluish light bounced along their roof. Finally, the Reeves family did what most people have done in such situations; they moved.

The Fortean context

Unlike the Bair incident, this Oregon case fits into the Fortean, paranormal, or ufological literature for a number of reasons. The series of events are called a "flap," an old Air Force term that has been applied to flying saucer and related accounts. The location is a special "spooky site"—a window area with a specific haunted history. The area served, if you will, as a "new port" for the phenomena. Once the manifestations began, it was as if the floodgates had opened. We see this again and again in such spooky sites as Pioneer Mountain.

Furthermore, the witnesses' name, Reeves, has been labeled as one of those special family titles that has been pinpointed as playing a magnetic role in the "name game." People named Reeves have a lot of strange experiences. These sightings were shared by so many people they have drifted nicely into the lore of weird places. But has the field of the unexplained become a series of conventionalizations itself?

Frankly, we have to come to grips with the concept it is really weird out there. And it's a lot weirder than it was yesterday. By now almost everyone has heard of UFOs, poltergeists, Ogopogo, Champ, and even the Jersey Devil. But there is an elaborately strange slew of entities and locations haunting the countryside. Even researchers into matters cryptozoological, paranormal, psychic, or otherwise strange, have been taken aback by the vast waves of critters and places that just do not fit into the usual world of the explained.

The Damned and the Undamned

Although the story is old hat by now, it serves as a quick illustration. Meteorites, literally stones from the skies, were not accepted as "real" for centuries by scientists. As Charles Fort, the modern founder of unexplained phenomena investigations, points out in his *The Book of the Damned*, a mere hundred and twenty years ago experts were trying to convince people that the stones from the skies were either the result of volcanic activity or whirlwinds. "Falling stones were damned." Now, of course, they are "undamned" and found in museums and textbooks. Earthquake lights, a past Fortean phenomena, are creeping into some textbooks. Cryptozoologically speaking, sea serpents, for example, have attained a sort of quasi-acceptance among biologist and zoologists; they are well on their way to becoming meteorites. You will soon meet in these pages a creature once thought to be only myth. But mostly what we are tracking down and what we are hearing from you is that there are things and sites even more bizarre than even an investigator of the unknown could have imagined a mere ten years ago.

Take Bigfeet. These hairy, eight-foot, man-like beasts were little heard of outside the Pacific Northwest before the work of John Green, Rene Dahinden, and Ivan Sanderson brought them to the attention of the reading public in the 1950s. By now, however, people have pigeonholed Bigfeet into a nice comfortable category, monsterwise, and have been less than enthusastic about other large hairy beasts that happened to turn up here and there. But they are popping up, in and out. In Pennsylvania, folks are seeing upright hairy things that look like werewolves. A couple of years ago, near York, Nebraska someone saw a satyr: a living, breathing Pan-like, goat-footed beastie. People around a village in Georgia recently saw a peg-legged Bigfoot. And around the Great Lakes, Mark A. Hall has gathered together an interesting bunch of reports of three-toed anthropoids.

Even the Loch Ness Monster seems tame nowadays. Off Virginia in the Potomac, a huge snake-like monster, "Chessie," has been routinely seen every summer since over thirty people saw "it" in 1978. And some of these witnesses are, we are told, Central Ingelligence Agency

(courtesy of the Institute of Fortean Studies)

As recently as the last century, widespread skepticism existed when people reported that stones fell from the skies. Scientists informed the public the "aerolites" must be the result of earthy explanations, such as volcanoes or whirlwinds. We now know meteorites are from outer space, and people reporting them are not crazy or lying. Although formerly "damned" phenomena, they are now "undamned" and well within the mainstream of scholarly investigations.

employees. Down along the Swanee River in Florida, a long-necked, gill-mouthed creature nicknamed "Pinkie" has become all the rage. In chapter 6, I will introduce you to the truly bizarre gillmen of the swampy Ohio River Valley. Researchers may believe they have to go to the Congo to hunt dinosaurs, but from my reading of the cases and discussions with hundreds of witnesses, some pretty strange stuff is to be found in our own backyards.

And More Curious Encounters in Mysterious America

In *Mysterious America*, I examined the phantasmagoria of black panthers, kangaroos, phantom clowns, alligators-in-the-sewers, mad gassers, and other engimas that have been a bit beyond the experiences of your everyday trek to the corner store. I continue that journey in this book. Little people, giant birds, sky serpents, phantom trains, mystery walls, and spooky spots will be some of the stops along the way. The world is mighty weird, and we can take some time and experience some of these wonders together.

Charles Fort, that clever researcher into matters inexplicable, once noted, the excluded and damned data "arrange themselves in mass-formations that pass and pass and keep on passing." We shall see that this Forteana, as it is now called in his honor (or his humorous dishonor, he might think), is not easy to place into neat little boxes. It's sort of like trying to put water in a bucket full of holes; once you get it in, before you know it, it's someplace else. Forteana's like that.

Don't be frustrated by the usual lack of explanations for this collection of sightings, stories, reports, and tales. Forteans are happy to gather the information together and engage in the game of presenting the data for the data's sake. I am, frankly, pleased I was able to just figure out some chapter headings that sort of made sense. And as you will soon discover, I have tried to point out some interesting patterns that seem to be underlying some of these stories. It's all a fun game, harmless, and done in good humor. Maybe a member of officialdom will come up with a nice lateral thinking explanation that will satisfactorily quiet the questions raised by these bits of nasty information. Maybe. But the reports will remain, just the same. The Fortean procession of the damned will continue. The circle, which one can start measuring anywhere, remains unbroken.

So now, on the road again, we shall go forth into the very strange world that is out there everyday, in broad daylight, and sometimes in the twilight. Let us share some encounters people have had a hard time discussing, but which seem to indicate another level of this existence we are just beginning to understand.

1

THE OCEANS
Mysteries from the Depths

The sea is the best field for data.—Charles Fort

Fort was correct. The vastness of the oceans has given us numerous examples of various mysteries. Some enigmas of the seas have been confronted, catalogued, and classified. Others have been dissected and discussed. Of course, the ones that intrigue us have been ignored and avoided.

The frequent and almost commonplace nature of sea monster stories, especially in bygone days, has made for a complacency of mind regarding such accounts. However, some rather uncommon elements remain in several of the reports. As portrayed in the next chapter, a few of these cross the line between animal and mechanical and raise many questions in our minds. Meanwhile, some travelers' tales of old have proven to be valid descriptions of creatures actually existing in the depths and point to hopes that other large unknown animals remain to be discovered. Still others, although somewhat similar to the reams of other such incidents, do demonstrate nuances of differences important to note.

A New England Sea Serpent

I investigated one of the latter types of reports early in 1985. Following an Appalachian Mountain Club talk I had given on cryptozoological material, I was cautiously approached by an elderly Scandinavian man. He pulled me aside, told me of a friend of his who had seen a "sea serpent," and wondered if I would want to speak to the gentleman. Needless to say, I was interested and took to tracking down this man's friend. Finally, I was able to catch up to Ole Mikkelsen, presently of Portland, Maine, and talk to him about his hair-raising meeting with a denizen of the deep.

I knew the sighting was not a recent one, so when I started to interview Mikkelsen, I expected some vague date as to when his encounter had occurred. Instead, the look in his eyes reminded me of another faraway stare I had seen before. It was that same glaze I have seen come over people alive in 1963 when asked where they were and what were they doing when John F. Kennedy was shot. Mikkelsen was reliving his experience right before me, and the date exploded from his lips. "The fifth day of June 1958! I won't soon forget it," he snapped. Before me sat a trim, muscular, tanned man of eighty-one. He told me he had been fishing since he was six years old and that he continued to do so up through last year. Born and raised in Denmark, he had come to Maine in 1923, and he knew the waters of Casco Bay well. But he had never met anything before 1958 to prepare him for the monster he saw that June.

The fifth had started like most work days for Mikkelsen back then. Up early, he and his since deceased partner, Egnar Haugaard, were out to sea before daybreak. On that June day, Mikkelsen recalled it was about one half hour after sunrise, about 6:00 A.M., when they first saw "it." They were about five miles off Cape Elizabeth, only about 1¼ miles south of the Portland Light Ship. Mikkelsen told me:

> Suddenly, we saw an object coming toward us out of a haze; we took it to be a submarine, but as it came near we discovered it was some live thing. As it came still nearer it dove down and a tail came up out of the water, and slowly it went down again. In about three or four minutes it surfaced again, came near us, and dove again. Then it came up once more about 125 feet away from us and stopped as if to look us over.

At that point, Haugaard shouted, "Give me the knife; if it comes nearer we will cut the nets and run for the lightship!"

"But luckily," Mikkelsen said, "it decided to swim in a nice turn to the south of us. We saw it disappear to the southeast in the haze."

Previously Unreported Behavior

Mikkelsen's metaphors were, not too surprisingly, ichthylogical. He told me the thing's color was like that of a cusk, a light-brown, North Atlantic food fish, with a less dark underside to its neck. He said the tail was like a mackerel's. But of course he knew it was not a cusk or a mackerel. What he saw was well over one hundred feet long, that he was sure of. The head he saw stuck out of the water and was broader than the long neck it was on. He could not pick out any ears or eyes, but he is certain it could hear.

Mikkelsen reported that every time the Portland Light Ship blew its mournful foghorn, as the anchored Coast Guard vessel did regularly, the creature turned its head in that direction. Haugaard and he had the thing in view for over forty-five minutes, and he constantly saw the creature's head rotating toward the sound of the lightship's horn.

A minor footnote in sea serpent lore, perhaps, but one that has never been remarked upon in the North Atlantic, according to one of the area's leading researchers, Gary Mangiacopra. I discussed the matter with him, and we both noted how classical sea serpent authors, such as Dr. Bernard Heuvelmans, Tim Dinsdale, Rupert Gould, and Dr. Anthonie Cornelis Oudemans, have suggested sea monster sightings are becoming rarer as a result of the increased noise in sealanes. And yet not one report of a sea serpent demonstrating hearing behavior has come forth, to our knowledge, before the one about which you just read.

Otherwise, the Mikkelsen report fits nicely into the growing body of reports dating back to the eighteenth century from the Northeast. Off Maine, in Broad Bay in 1751 and in Penobscot Bay in 1779, sea serpents were sighted by men fishing the same waters as Mikkelsen. During June and July 1818, fishermen told of seeing a sea serpent in Portland Harbor. Many sightings occurred off Woods Island, Maine in the early 1900s. Eastport, Maine was the scene of encounters in the late 1930s and in 1940. The 1958 case merely extends this legacy.

The Many-humped Sea Serpent

In *Mysterious America*, I illustrated a mention of the famed nineteenth-century Gloucester, Massachusetts sea monster with a copy of an old woodprint showing this great unknown. That representation does not generally match what Mikkelsen saw. But Heuvelmans' drawing of the typical New England monster, which he entitled "The Many-humped Sea-serpent," looks very much like Mikkelsen's description of the serpent he saw. For example, Heuvelmans' serpent's tail is "bilobate like the cetacean's"; indeed, Mikkelsen's "mackerel tail" would look exactly like a skinny version of the flukes of a whale. This bit of detail in the description would also agree with Gary Mangiacopra's and Dr. Roy Mackal's theories that these animals are zeuglodens, or primitive whales.

The Portland, Maine resident appears to have had a rather ordinary sighting of a New England sea serpent, but he was lucky enough to have witnessed a rather extraordinary detail of its behavior. The beast exhibited it could hear. Someday if the sea serpent becomes as undamned as the meteorite, this observation of Ole Mikkelsen may help in understanding further these creatures of the oceans.

Monster Architeuthids

In the past, witnesses' stories and seafarers' accounts have foreshadowed later insights about new animals. Testimony to this is the story of the giant squid, *Architeuthis*. Only recently accepted into the world of marine biology, we know of these creatures from the tales of ancient Greece's *Scylla*, Norway's *Kraken*, and Patagonia's *Cornet*. Fictionalized in admittedly sensational terms in Jules Verne's *20,000 Leagues Under the Sea* and Melville's *Moby Dick*, the giant squid has been marvelled by our ancestors, just as we hold the Loch Ness Monster in awe today.

There is some reason, however, for the continued reverence of the giant squid in modern times. *Architeuthis* is rarely seen and perhaps is the most mysterious invertebrate in nature. Only one hundred giant squid have ever been encountered, and usually these were ones that have been found dead. I was able to talk to the people involved with the most recent North American stranding and learn more about this only recently accepted monster of the sea.

Early in February 1980, a giant squid washed ashore on Plum Island, Massachusetts. Giant squid had not been seen near the Bay State since 1909, and its discovery here was one of those events for

(courtesy of Bernard Heuvelmans)

Casco Bay, Maine. Ole Mikkelsen's description of a large monster he saw near Cape Elizabeth, Maine, in 1958, matches closely the composite drawing Dr. Bernard Heuvelmans has created from several sightings of similar unknown animals seen off the New England coast. Heuvelmans calls this animal "The Many-humped Sea-serpent." Mikkelsen was able to observe a behavior never before reported for these sea serpents.

which naturalists wait a lifetime. That this specimen of *Architeuthis* should land on the well-protected sands of the Parker River National Wildlife Refuge took everyone by surprise—normally, the Plum Island sanctuary is a tranquil haunt for beachcombers and bird watchers. Al Zelly, assistant refuge manager, described the discovery to me this way:

> It was a cold, February-type day. William Patoulias, one of our enforcement officers, was on a routine patrol in his jeep that morning. He was surveying the beach, as he regularly does, for 'protection and control' purposes; you see, most of our involvement and enforcement is with humans. Anyway, suddenly, three and a half miles down the beach, he saw it.

What Patoulias saw was a 450-pound, cream-colored, tentacled pile of squid.

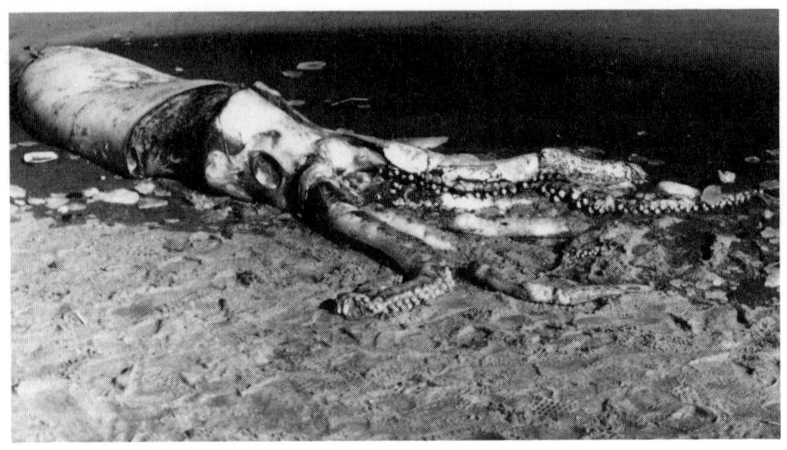

(photograph by Carla Skinder)

Plum Island, Massachusetts. The giant squid that beached here in 1980 was only a shadow of its former self, but it weighed in at almost a quarter of a ton. This gigantic monster of the sea was formerly known only from the tales and myths of sea-faring nations. Was the Massachusetts stranding a hint to the mystery of the thirty-year cycle of appearances of these creatures? Will the 1990s produce a wave of sightings of these animals and sea serpents?

Zelly continued:

William came and got me, and we pretty quickly figured out what it was. I was familiar with the small squids from catching them in the Pacific, and to me, this thing just looked like a bigger version of the same thing. Frankly, I was not too excited because at the time I did not know it was that rare of a find. But I thought the people at the New England Aquarium would be interested. They came out, and a crew of us lifted the squid onto a stretcher and put it into a pickup. Then the Aquarium people transferred it to a waiting van. They took the giant squid into Boston and put it on display.

I don't know that much about them, but I think it is rare for these squid to wash up in populated areas. If it would have come up on some other beach, on an isolated one, the right people would not have seen it, would not have noticed it, recognized, or appreciated it. I now realize how rare and unique this beaching was.

The Plum Island giant squid had lost part of its great mass in its rough death and beaching. Although its body measured some eight feet in length, plus eight more feet of battered tentacles, the two long whiplike tentacles and the ends of all the others were missing. Dr. Kenneth J. Boss, a Harvard University biology professor with a special interest in mollusk zoology, told me that the tentacles may have been eaten off before the giant squid had finally settled on the sand. Dr. Clyde Roper, a curator for the Smithsonian Institution who flew in to examine the creature, ventured that it had probably measured thirty feet in length.

Little Understood Giants

Giant squids are, of course, closely related to the common, little squids so often used in Japanese and Italian cuisine. The scale is larger, but the body parts are the same—saucer-sized lidless eyes, parrotlike beak, strong suction cups on the two giant whiplike arms, and eight tentacles. Like its smaller relatives, the giant squid moves by jet-stream propulsion and is capable of squirting out the classic cloud of ink in defense just like its cousin, the octopus. Despite the efforts of Jacques-Yves Cousteau and other marine explorers, not a great deal more has been learned about the giant squid since the days of the *Kraken*. Today's naturalists do not even know exactly what these squids eat; when specimens like the Plum Island example are discovered, their stomachs are usually empty.

Much of our information on the giant squid comes from old sailing-record accounts of sperm whale kills and the often amazing contents of their stomachs. In 1895, Prince Albert of Monaco described the events following the killing of one such whale:

> The ship (was) now afloat in a hectare of reddish water, through which ran rivulets of a deeper hue as blood poured from the animal. The more intense color was dissipated, then blended into various tints, as clouds coming down from the mountains are confounded with fog on the plains.
>
> The whale's gigantic head was alongside our stern, and its lower jaw, hanging loose now that the muscles had relaxed, was moved by the actions of the waves. I could see the mouth, like a yawning cavern. And I saw it vomit out, one after another, the bodies of several cephalopods—

> octopuses or squids—of colossal size. These, apparently, were the fruits of the whale's final plunge to the depths, following which it had been harpooned on the surface, (and) a recent meal which had, as yet, hardly been affected by digestion.

Prince Albert had his naturalists gather the contents of this and other whales' stomachs. Remarking on the studies of the "unpleasant mass," Prince Albert noted: "Toward the end, the naturalists' stomachs revolted in a faint echo of the event which the day before had given these treasures to science during the final spasms of the dying whale."

Prince Albert's scholars described many unknown species of giant squid as the result of their thorough, though distasteful, examinations. Others have made similar finds. One of the largest giant squids on record, a sixty-five footer, was discovered in the stomach of a sperm whale.

Strandings and Theories

Beachings of giant squid in the Northeast are uncommon, but not unheard of. In Bernard Heuvelmans' expansive and excellent book on the subject, *In the Wake of the Sea Serpent: The Kraken and the Giant Squid*, he chronicles a series of strandings and sightings of giant squid on and near Newfoundland and Labrador from 1871 to 1879. Heuvelmans noted that one giant squid was recorded to have had an arm measuring forty-two feet in length. Some sixty of the Newfoundland giants had been cut up for cod bait before they could be examined. Others were eaten by fish and gulls. The few that were properly inspected included the biggest stranded squid ever accepted by science—the Thimble Tickle specimen—with a body twenty feet long, arms thirty-five feet long, eyes eighteen inches across, and a beak nine inches in diameter. Gerald L. Wood, author of the *Guinness Book of Animal Facts and Feats*, has told Gary Mangiacopra that he figures the Thimble Tickle squid that beached in November of 1878 probably weighed about four thousand pounds.

Theories abound regarding the squid deaths of which Heuvelmans writes. Some feel a possible explanation may lie in the "cold wall" where the frigid Labrador Current meets the Gulf Stream. Researcher G.C. Robson found that giant squid seek a water temperature of about fifty degrees; if a squid crosses the cold wall, it will naturally try to rise nearer the surface in a futile effort to reach warmer water and will die of cold. This may have been the cause of the Plum Island squid's death. Continental weather changed radically around the first of February 1980 to a more normal winter pattern for the Northeast. The six previous weeks of moderate, dry temperatures may have seduced the giant squid into going farther north than it ordinarily would have; after the weather change, the squid may have been caught in colder waters and died.

Past Cycles: Preview of the Future?

Another interesting theory for the squid deaths comes from Dr. Frederick A. Aldrich, professor of zoology at Memorial University, in St. John, Newfoundland. Aldrich surveyed the records of past strandings and sightings of giant squid along the eastern Canadian coast, and came up with an amazing discovery. The decade of the 1870s was a period of numerous encounters with the giant squids, in the sea and on the beaches. It was not until the Reverend Mr. Moses Harvey first collected one in 1873 that the giant squids moved from the shadowy world of legends and myth to that of marine science. But Aldrich dug deeper and found that the meetings with the squids also peaked in the decade of 1900-1910 and in the 1930s. Noting the period of encounters were usually in the autumn, Aldrich theorized a thirty-year cycle of giant squid occurrences in the waters of Newfoundland. During the 1960s, based upon his hypothesis, Aldrich told me, "I have been able to secure over fifteen Architeuthids washed ashore in Newfoundland and apparently as a function of my theory with respect to the Labrador current." Aldrich, therefore, believes the next wave of beachings in the western North Atlantic will occur in the 1990s. Perhaps the Plum Island squid was an advance preview. Certainly, we note the beachings worldwide may be going into a period of increased activity. Early in February of 1985, Japan reported a giant squid was found on one of their beaches.

Related Wonders Await

Whatever happens in the future, the 1980 beaching of a giant squid on Plum Island was a rarity, and the New England Aquarium understood that when it put the squid on display. Many Bostonians and visitors peered at what probably seemed an eighth wonder of the natural world. The Aquarium's public relations spokesperson, Liz Kay, told me the response was so overwhelming that they extended the creature's stay for several weeks beyond the original month. But the time finally came, late in the spring of 1980, when the giant squid had to find permanent housing, and the Aquarium shipped it over to Harvard's Museum of Comparative Zoology, and then it was taken to the Smithsonian's Museum of Natural History. For over a year, in Washington, D.C., the public was able to view a true sea monster. Many gazed at a wonder few people have seen. Even Jules Verne, who wrote of the giant "poulps" with such emotion in his *20,000 Leagues Under the Sea*, apparently never viewed one firsthand. Verne obtained his squid material from reading the Norwegian legend of the *Kraken*.

During the next decade, if Frederick Aldrich is correct, others in the Northeast may soon have contact with these formerly mythical creatures. For while the still "undiscovered" relatives of the giant squid—the Lusca of the blue holes of Andros and the giant octopus of the Bahamas—continue to occupy that shadowy world of cryptozoology along with the many-humped sea serpent, marine biologists have had to, at least, admit the legendary *Kraken* is more fact than fiction.

The sea is a wonderful field for data.

2

THE SEA AND THE AIR
Sea Machines and Sky Serpents

We are not realists. We are not idealists. We are intermediatists—that nothing is real, but that nothing is unreal: that all phenomena are approximations one way or the other between realness and unrealness. —*Charles Fort*

In recent years the papers have been filled with stories of unidentified submarines off the coast of Norway and Sweden. Now perhaps several of these accounts have issued from the comings and goings of Russian submarines. As readers of *Newsweek* or *Time* may know, one submarine did beach in Hars Bay, Sweden in October of 1982. But the stories of USOs, "unidentified submerged objects," go back many years before the recent era of the East/West Cold War. More often than not, these USOs are characterized in the literature as "underwater UFOs," and they do seem to have been with us for decades. For example, reports of a major USO flap were recorded during the 1940s off the coast of Greenland, as well as in the seas around Sweden, according to John Keel. Elsewhere, USO activity has popped up in such diverse American locales as: New Orleans, 1954; Jacksonville, Florida, 1957; Bodega Bay, California, 1958; Portsmouth, New Hampshire, 1959; New York City, 1960; Port Aransas, Texas, 1961; and Portland, Maine, 1963. The area near Fort Pierce and Homestead, Florida experienced a mini-flap of USO reports in 1965 to 1966.

USOs of Yesteryears

But as I have discovered from some interesting reexaminations of old accounts, the so-called USOs of today may have been chronicled as something strangely familiar in the past.

From the journal the *Zoologist* and London's *Daily Mail*, we have the curious detailing of the 28 October 1902 encounter between the steamship *Fort Salisbury* and something seemingly beyond the crew's understanding. The lookout reported that there was a huge, dark object bearing two lights in the sea ahead. The steamship "passed about forty to fifty yards on the port side of the wake," according to the second officer, Raymer. The ship's personnel estimated the "object" was between five hundred and six hundred feet in length. As Charles Fort emphasized when he commented on this Atlantic Ocean sighting in his classic book *Lo!*, the observers thought that mechanisms of some kind, fins perhaps, were making a commotion in the sea. "A scaled back," Fort noted, was slowly submerging.

It was the mention of the "scaled back" that most interested Fort, and most interests us. Fort wrote, "So doubly damned is this datum that the attempt to explain it was in terms of the accursed Sea Serpent." Indeed, later cryptozoologists have not been kind to this report. Bernard Heuvelmans in his book *In the Wake of the Sea-Serpents* calls the story "all nonsense." But one thinks immediately of the *Nautilus*, Captain Nemo's submarine, in Jules Verne's celebrated *20,000 Leagues Under the Sea*, (first published in 1870), a vessel whose appearance was designed to make those who encountered it believe they had seen some kind of strange sea monster. Verne's tale is a grand mix of Fortean facts and the author's imagination.

Insights of Jules Verne

Verne gives away his depth of knowledge in his brief passage on the discussions occurring because of the many sightings of the creature. "In every place of great resort the monster was the fashion. They sang of it in the cafes, ridiculed it in the papers, and represented it on the stage.... The legends of ancient times were even resuscitated, and the opinions of Aristotle and Pliny revived, who admitted the existence of these monsters, as well as the Norwegian tales of Bishop Pontoppidan, the accounts of Paul Heggede, and, last of all, the reports of

Mr. Harrington (whose good faith no one could suspect) who affirmed that, being on board the *Castillan* in 1857, he had seen this enormous serpent."

Jules Verne nicely illustrated, in his graphic introduction of the animal-like qualities of the *Nautilus*, the shadowy world between machine and monster, which perhaps he had discovered from his research into such encounters as that between the *Fort Salisbury* and its unknown visitor.

Verne was a compulsive collector of curiosa, just like Fort, and seems to have based some of his ideas on accounts of what later would be termed Fortean phenomena. For example, *Clipper of the Clouds* and *Master of the World*, two related "Robur" novels, apparently were inspired by mid-nineteenth-century French reports of a mysterious "airship." For more on the United States reports of 1800s "airships" see Jerome Clark's and my book, *The Unidentified* (Warner, 1975) or the more skeptical *The Great Airship Mystery* (Dodd, Mead & Co., 1981) by Daniel Cohen.

Puget Sound Monster or Machine?

A related and rather incredible event allegedly took place nine years before the *Fort Salisbury* incident in the northwestern part of the United States—not far from the area where the first great modern UFO wave erupted in 1947. The supposed witnesses, William Fitzhenry, H.L. Beal, W.L. McDonald, J.K. Bell, Henry Blackwood, and two "eastern gentlemen" who asked that their names not be used, had left in the sloop *Marion* on a fishing expedition in Puget Sound just prior to the experience. The following account was published in the *Tacoma* (Washington) *Daily Ledger* for 3 July 1893:

> We left Tacoma about 4:30 P.M., Saturday, July 1st, and as the wind was from the southeast we shaped our course for Point Defiance, intending to anchor off that point and try our luck with rod and line. We cast anchor about six o'clock, the wind having died out, and had fair success fishing. The wind coming up again pretty strong Mr. McDonald suggested getting under way for Black Fish Bay, Henderson Island, as he knew of a fine trout stream running into the bay and also an excellent camping place near the fishing ground.

So about eight o'clock we weighed anchor and shaped our course for Black Fish Bay, which place we reached about 9:30. We landed and made everything snug about the boat and made a nice camp on shore, and as it was by this time eleven o'clock we all turned in to get a little sleep as it was agreed upon that at the first streak of daylight we should all get up. About one hundred yards from our camp was the camp of a surveying party, but as it was so late we decided that we would not disturb them but that we would call upon them the following morning and would probably get some valuable pointers as to the best places to fish and hunt on the island. After a few jokes had been cracked, the boys laid down, and in a short time everything about camp became as still as death.

It was, I guess, about midnight before I fell asleep, but exactly how long I slept I cannot say, for when I woke it was with such startling suddenness that it never entered my mind to look at my watch, and when after a while I did look at my watch, as well as every watch belonging to the party, it was stopped.

I am afraid that you will fail to comprehend how suddenly that camp was awake.

Since the creation of the world I doubt if sounds and sights more horrible were ever seen or heard by mortal man. I was in the midst of a pleasant dream, when in an instant a most horrible noise rang out in the clear morning air, and instantly the whole air was filled with a strong current of electricity that caused every nerve in the body to sting with pain, and a light as bright as that created by the concentration of many arc lights kept constantly flashing. At first I thought it was a thunderstorm, but as no rain accompanied it, and as both light and sound came from off the bay, I turned my head in that direction, and if it is possible for fright to turn one's hair white, then mine ought to be snow white, for right before my eyes was a most horrible-looking monster.

By this time every man in our camp, as well as the men from the camp of the surveyors, was gathered on the bank of the stream; and as soon as we could gather our wits together we began to question if what we were looking at was not the creation of the mind. But we were soon disburdened of this idea, for the monster slowly drew in toward the shore, and as it approached, from its head poured out a stream of water that looked like blue fire. All the while the air seemed to be filled with electricity, and the sensation experienced was as if each man had on a suit of clothes formed of the fine points of needles.

One of the men from the surveyors' camp incautiously took a few steps in the direction of the water that reached the man, and he instantly fell to the ground and lay as though dead.

Mr. McDonald attempted to reach the man's body to pull it back into a place of safety, but he was struck with some of the water that the monster was throwing and fell senseless to the earth. By this time every man in both parties was panic-stricken, and we rushed to the woods for a place of safety, leaving the fallen men lying on the beach.

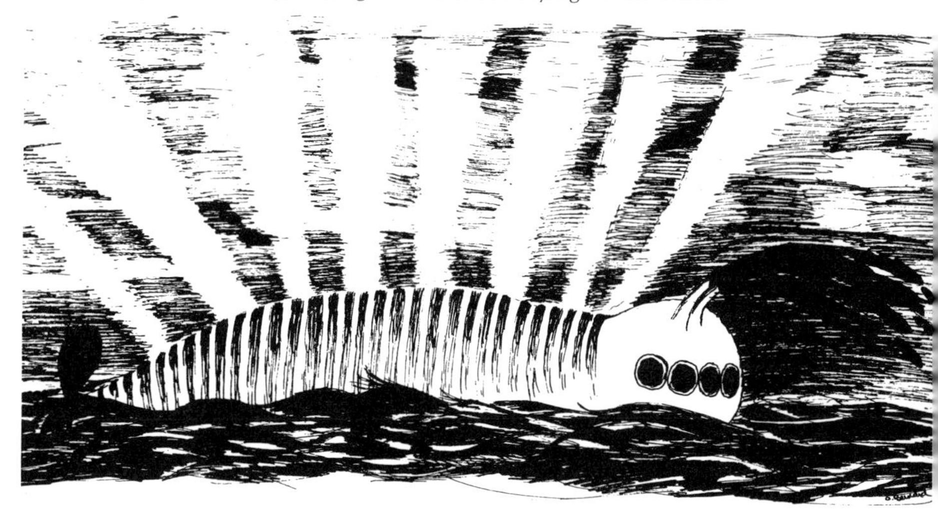

(drawing by Anne Bernard for the Institute of Fortean Studies)

Black Fish Bay, Puget Sound, Washington. The incredible 1893 meeting between a strange ocean-going "machine" and seven unsuspecting fishermen is captured in this graphic impression of the event. According to the witnesses of the time, the sea machine appeared like a "demon of the deep," poured "blue fire" from the "horns" at its front, and filled the air with electricity. Measuring over one hundred fifty feet long, the thing was covered with what appeared to be copper bands. From these bands came the powerful electric force that stopped the men's watches and produced bright rays of illumination. It seems to have been driven by a propeller-shaped "tail." Although the event seems like part of a Jules Verne story, it is one of the nonfictional sightings of unidentified submerged objects, USOs.

As we reached the woods the 'demon of the deep' sent out flashes of light that illuminated the surrounding country for miles, and his roar—which sounded like the roar of thunder—became terrific. When we reached the woods we looked around and saw the monster making off in the direction of the sound, and in an instant it disappeared beneath the waters of the bay, but for some time we were able to trace its course by a bright luminous light that was on the surface of the water. As the fish disappeared, total darkness surrounded us, and it took us some time to find our way back to the beach where our comrades lay. We were unable to tell the time, as the powerful electric force had stopped our watches. We eventually found McDonald and the other man and were greatly relieved to find that they were alive, though unconscious. So we sat down to await the coming of daylight. It came, I should judge, in about half an hour, and by this time, by constant work on the two men, both were able to stand.

This monster fish, or whatever you may call it, was fully 150 feet long, and at its thickest part I should judge about 30 feet in circumference. Its shape was somewhat out of the ordinary insofar that the body was neither round nor flat but oval, and from what we could see the upper part of the body was covered a very coarse hair. The head was shaped very much like the head of a walrus, though, of course, very much larger. Its eyes, of which it apparently had six, were as large around as a dinner plate and were exceedingly dull, and it was about the only spot on the monster that at one time or another was not illuminated. At intervals of about every eight feet from its head to its tail a substance that had the appearance of a copper band encircled its body, and it was from these many bands that the powerful electric current appeared to come. The bands nearest the head seemed to have the strongest electric force, and it was from the first six bands that the most brilliant lights were emitted. Near the center of its head were two large horn-like substances, though they could not have been horns for it was through them that the electrically charged water was thrown.

Its tail from what I could see of it was shaped like a propeller and seemed to revolve, and it may be possible that the strange monster pushes himself through the water by means of this propeller-like tail. At will this strange monstrosity seemed to be able to emit strong waves of electric current, giving off electro-motive forces, which causes any person coming within the radius of this force to receive an electric shock ....

> I hardly need to tell you that we were not long in getting under way for Tacoma, and I can assure you that I have no further desire to fish any more in the waters of this bay. There are too many peculiar inhabitants in them. I am going to send a full account of our encounter to the Smithsonian Institute, and I doubt not but what they will send out some scientific chaps to investigate.

Clearly, if this fantastic story is true, we are dealing with some sort of machine-like contrivance that has assumed the shape of a sea monster. The electromagnetic effects, the lights, the copper bands, and the propeller all make this an inescapable conclusion, despite some fanciful theorizing at the time to the effect that this might be a giant mutant fish.

Sky Unclassifiables

The problem of making sense of such accounts becomes even more difficult when we come upon reports of weird aerial constructions like one seen near Copiapo, Chile in 1868 and cited by Fort from *Zoologist* for July of the same year. The object carried lights and was driven by a noisy motor, or as a contemporary source described it, "a gigantic bird; eyes wide open and shining like burning coals; covered with immense scales, which clashed together with a metallic sound." Almost a hundred years later, near Point Pleasant, West Virginia, John A. Keel would investigate the reports of the giant bird-like creature, Mothman and comment on its uncanny ability to fly about without flapping its wings. Keel felt something more mechanical than monstrous was about. And in my investigations of the huge, winged weirdie seen by Thomas Downy some ten years later in the Bridgewater Triangle (a location of focused unexplained activity in Massachusetts; see *Mysterious America*, chapter 4), the same machine-like quality issued from the story the policeman told me.

Even more to the point is a story from the Bonham, Texas, *Enterprise*, which noted that during June 1873, a local resident "saw something resembling an enormous serpent" floating above his farm. Others working nearby saw it too and were understandably unnerved. "It seemed to be as large and long as a telegraph pole, (and) was of a yellow striped color." The men could see the serpent "coil itself up, turn over, and thrust forward its huge head as if striking at something." Shortly thereafter, according to the *New York Times* of 7 July 1873, a similar phenomenon appeared over Fort Scott, Kansas, "halfway above the horizon." Witnesses stated, "a huge serpent, apparently perfect in form, was plainly seen."

Fort further notes a serpent "flap" in Darlington County, South Carolina, in May 1888. This time the thing supposedly made a "hissing sound." Other reports, with which Fort was unfamiliar, include the following: On 5 December 1762 a "twisting serpent" lit up the English town of Bideford, Devon, for six minutes before fading away, and a "serpent of fire" taking the form of a horseshoe passed over Geneva on 15 May 1811. It was also seen in Paris.

In more modern times, March 1935, something described as "a large shining form resembling a gigantic snake wriggling forth in the northwestern sky" appeared over southern Norway and Denmark. It is said to have had four or five curves and to have moved in a vertical position with its "head" pointed toward the earth. Back in the Americas, a similar object was observed twice over Cruz Alta, Brazil, in December of the same year. When it reappeared in July 1937 its "head" had become a ball of fire.

Last Century's Great Scare

Then there was the Great Scare of 1857-1858, when in the late dusk one evening a giant serpent hovered above a steamboat slowing for a landing along the Missouri River in Nebraska. It seemed to be breathing fire, say accounts, and it had "lighted streaks" along its sides. Sightings must have continued, for some years later a song passed into local folk tradition:

> 'Twas a dark night in Sixty-six
> When we was layin' steel
> We seen a flyin' engine come
> Without no wing or wheel
> It came a-roarin' in the sky
> With lights along the side ...
> And scales like a serpent's hide.

By the turn of the century Nebraskans were no longer confusing serpents and UFOs. In February 1897 the mystery "airships" had begun flying over the state, and in the years ahead stories were revived of a giant creature in the waters of Alkali Lake near Hay Springs (first told by the Native Americans to the first white settlers in the area). One observer said that "its head was like an oil barrel, shiny black in the moonlight. Its flashing green eyes were spitting fire."

With incidents recounted like these in this chapter, we are moving into new and uncharted territory, where the line between "machines" and "animals" becomes blurred, as, indeed, does the line that divides the various types of Fortean phenomena. The moral may be that research that concentrates on UFOs or monsters alone and ignores the other mysteries of the physical world is somewhat shortsighted.

3

THE SKY
Thunderbirds

There are extraordinary occurrences and conventionalization cloaks them, and the more commonplace the cloakery, the more satisfactory. —Charles Fort

Native Americans were excellent chroniclers of the natural world. They often spoke, in great depth and across tribal groups, about giant flying creatures they called "thunderbirds."

The familiar word has now become part of America's modern culture, denoting everything from a very cheap wine to a classic automobile. Most people associate the maker of thunder as a part of past Old West legends. However many Cheyennes, Arapahos, Comanches, and other Native Americans claim to actually have seen one or more thunderbirds during their lives. To the Native Americans, the birds were more than mythological creatures; the thunderbirds were real animals. And reports of real thunderbirds continue today.

Illinois' Postwar Thunderbirds

Although the sightings of these massive feathered wonders have occurred from west to east, I find it much more illustrative to concentrate on one hotspot of accounts. A particularly interesting cluster of thunderbird sightings have issued from the state of Illinois. As I mentioned in *Mysterious America*, one of the most bizarre big bird cases of all time involved the attempted abduction of ten-year-old Marlon Lowe from his Logan County, Illinois frontyard. My brother, Jerry, and I interviewed the principals in the case during 1977 and 1979, and we continue to accept that a couple of enormous birds did pluck the boy from the ground, only to drop him within seconds. But the Lowe case is not the first big bird report from that state. Digging through newspaper achives more than a quarter of a century ago, I was able to discover a whole series of sightings for 1948.

For the press, it all began on 9 April 1948 on a farm outside Caledonia, Illinois, when Mr. and Mrs. Robert Price saw what they called "a monster bird . . . bigger than an airplane." It had a long neck, huge powerful wings, and in Robert Price's words, "what I suppose were its feet trailing behind it." It flew out of sight toward the northeast.

Shortly afterwards, a Freeport, Illinois truck driver came forth with corroborating testimony admitting that he had seen the huge creature from a different location on the same day. "I saw the bird," Veryl Babb said, "but at first I didn't say anything because I thought people would laugh at me. When I read that Price had seen it I decided to report all about it."

And then a former army colonel related that nearly a week before, on 4 April, a gigantic bird had passed four thousand feet above him while he stood talking with Colonel Ralph Jackson, head of Western Military Academy, and a farmer near Alton, Illinois. He did not point it out to his companions. He said, "it looked too incredible. I thought there was something wrong with my eyesight," Walter F. Siegmund, wartime commander of the Kearns, Utah Army Air Force base, said, "but it was definitely a bird and not a glider or jet plane. It appeared to be flying northeast. Two Army planes had just flown over in the same direction, and I thought it was a pursuit craft following them. But from the movements of the object and its size, I figured it could only be a bird of some tremendous size."

Old Cases Revived

Because of the interest and possible acceptance of these strange stories of big birds seen in the sky, an even older story turned up. It

(courtesy of the Institute of Fortean Studies)

Midwestern Skies. The descriptions of the Illinois' thunderbirds closely match what one would expect a giant Andean condor would look like flying around the Midwest. The Andean condor's white ruffed neck is often a part of the witnesses' narratives; the all-black body and neck of the only North American condor, the California condor, do not fit what people have reported. Here, both birds are seen in their resting postures.
Condors are rare birds, and a South American bird in Illinois would be an even scarcer visitor. Is the answer to be found in the fossil remains of a prehistoric North American near-relative that resembles the Andean condor?

was a twelve-year-old boy named James Trares, who first sighted the mysterious bird, but only his parents and he had discussed the details. Now, the Trares went to the papers with their story. Three months before, in January 1948, James was playing outside his parents' Monier Drive home in Glendale, Illinois, just before sunset. Suddenly, he saw something that sent him scurrying inside to his mother, Mrs. J.J. Trares. "There's a bird outside as big as a B-29!", he exclaimed breathlessly. He said he knew it was not a plane because he saw its wings flapping. The creature was gray-green in color and flying toward the sun. The Trares story, and an earlier one from Ramore, Ontario, may indicate the big bird was around long before the April reports.

Anyway, the reports did continue.

In the Midst of a Flap

On 10 April 1948, the day after the Price and Babb sightings in Caledonia, the bird appeared over Overland, Illinois and was sighted by Mr. and Mrs. Clyde C. Smith and Les Bacon. They said they thought it was a pursuit plane until it began to flap its wings furiously. The big bird appeared to be dark gray in color from where they viewed it in the Smiths' backyard just before noon. As it happened, it was Clyde Smith's second sighting of the day. "I first saw it when I was out in the yard that morning," he said later, "and I thought it was a type of plane I had never seen before. It was circling and banking in a way I had never seen a plane perform, and I kept waiting for it to fall."

A week later, on the eighteenth, Chet Burke of Richmond Heights, Illinois, reported that a strange bird passed over his house. But this one was much smaller than a plane and resembled an albatross, a seabird with a seven-foot wingspan that does not ever come as far inland as western Illinois. In fact, albatross have never officially been seen west of Maine.

On 24 April a more impressive report was made at Alton, Illinois where E. M. Coleman and his fifteen-year-old son James gazed on an astonishing sight. "It was an enormous, incredible thing with a body that looked like a naval torpedo," E.M. Coleman said. "It was flying at about five hundred feet and cast a shadow the same size as that of a Piper Cub at the same height."

Patrolmen Clarence Johnson and Francis Hennelly of the St. Louis Police Department got a look at the bird as it flew silhouetted against the moon that same night. "The thing was as big as a small airplane," Hennelly said. "Its wings were flapping, and it was headed southwest, flying at an altitude of several hundred feet. I thought it was a large eagle, but I've never seen one that big before."

Dr. Dolezal's Description

Two days later, on 26 April 1948, a St. Louis chiropractor, Dr. Kristine Dolezal, had just finished breakfasting in her second floor apartment. About 8:40 A.M. she got up from the table and started across the kitchen. Suddenly the sounds of a nearby airplane flying low over the house broke the silence. "It sounded like something was wrong with the motor," Dr. Dolezal commented later. "It sort of roared and sputtered." She stepped out onto the porch to see what was wrong but was hardly prepared for what greeted her. "I looked at the plane, then I glanced over the other way," she reported. "I saw this bird just come from nowhere it seemed like. I thought, What is it? Is it a big bird, or what?" As the creature came nearer it seemed inexplicably to grow larger. Dr. Dolezal at first thought her eyes were playing tricks on her, but then she realized it had spread its wings, which previously had been folded back. In the meantime, the plane changed course, and for a moment it looked like the bird and plane were about to collide. But the bird flapped its wings lazily three times, and both bird and plane vanished into the clouds.

In the 2 May 1948 issue of the *St. Louis Post Dispatch's* "Everyday Magazine," writer Dickson Terry noted, "Like others who have seen the thing, Dr. Dolezal describes it as grayish-black in color. Her description of the deliberate beating of the huge wings also jibes with other descriptions. However, where others describe it as having no tail to speak of, the thing she saw had, she says, quite an exceptional tail. It was like a rectangular box which had been sawed or divided down the center. When its (wings) were spread, she said, she could see ridges across them, like the ribs which show beneath the covering on the wings of a plane."

The following day, instructors at the Mississippi School of Aeronautics at Lambert-St. Louis Field sighted an "awfully big bird" at an altitude of about twelve hundred feet.

Little more than twenty-four hours later salesman Harry Bradford, while in the process of turning off the Red Feather Express Highway at Kings Highway, saw the bird, stopped his car, and turned a spotlight on it. The creature circled for a moment or two, then streaked northward, "I've seen it three times in the last four days, and that's too much tomfoolery for a man of fifty to take," Bradford told the press.

Hertenstein's Heron and Other Explanations

Apparently it was getting to be too much for other persons as well, if the letters stacking up in the St. Louis Mayor Aloys P. Kaufmann's office were any indication. "Why has nothing been done about this?" one letter writer demanded to know. "All St. Louis is upset about it. Who knows? Maybe it's a man-killing bird." Another wrote, "I don't think it's a bird—but I hope it is." Still others offered theories: it was an albatross, a blue heron, a pelican—unlikely "explanations" considering the reported behavior and size of the big bird. The explanations, therefore, began to become as bizarre as the sightings themselves. Officials were leaning over backwards to quiet the furor.

The mayor, for his part, passed the buck to his administrative assistant, Charles Hertenstein, who was given instructions (apparently seriously) to set a trap for the beast. However, after discovering blue heron tracks on an island in the Meramec River on the thirtieth, Hertenstein, relieved, suggested this might be the explanation—although the reports had suggested a considerably larger bird than the blue heron, a common enough sight along the Illinois-Missouri border.

But the Sightings Continue

The next day Hertenstein's sigh of relief had turned into a groan. "Don't tell me we now have a self-illuminated flying monster," he complained. But that is precisely what three St. Louis citizens, Charles Dunn, a U.S. Steel inspector, his wife Mary, and Clifford Warden, had reported seeing the night before at ten o'clock. Said Charles Dunn, "I thought people who reported the thing were seeing 'bugs' until I looked into the sky last night. It was flapping its wings and moving quite fast at about three thousand feet altitude and appeared to be illuminated by a dull glow. It looked about the size of a Piper Cub plane, but there was no engine sound, and it was not a plane. I could hardly believe my eyes."

At this juncture the Civil Air Patrol offered to make aerial searches for the bird whose appearances had begun to attract national attention. A man from Bowling Green, Indiana, wrote Hertenstein to tell him he had seen it or something very similar two years before, and it had been the size of a twelve-hundred-pound horse. Albert T.

Bertram, Jr., a meteorological aide with the U.S. Weather Bureau, describing his 2 May sighting, said the bird resembled the storks he had seen in Africa.

Then on May fifth, the glowing, giant bird paid its last 1948 visit to the St. Louis-Alton area. Arthur Davidson, a candy broker of University City, Missouri, called the police at 9:05 P.M. to say he had seen it. He noted "it was greyish and illuminated . . . . It seemed to be flying over the old folk's home." At 10:30 P.M., Mrs. William Stallings of nearby St. Louis informed the authorities that she and her husband had seen it. "It was bright, about as big as a house. It was greenish-yellow and bobbed up and down," Stallings said.

Ironically, just when the public excitement reached its peak the sightings came to an abrupt end.

The Piasa and Kin

To the Native Americans of the area the giant mystery birds were really nothing new. Their traditions are filled with stories about the *Piasa*. The French explorer Marquette was the first European to describe this legendary creature, for the Illini had left an artistic representation of it for all to see. Marquette wrote:

> On the flat face of a high rock were painted, in red, black, and green, a pair of monsters, each as large as a calf, with horns like a deer, red eyes, a beard like a tiger, and a frightful expression of countenance. The face is something like that of a man, the body covered with scales, and the tail so long that it passes entirely round the body, over the head, and between the legs, ending like that of a fish.

An Alton, Illinois scholar named McAdams, observed during the mid-1800s, that the name Piasa "signifies, in Illini, 'The bird which devours men.'" According to legend, the giant bird had its home high in a cave in the bluff. In the beginning, it was able to coexist with the Illini, but during a battle between two tribes, the Piasa carried away two warriors, feasted on them, and acquired a liking for human flesh. Soon children and adults were carried away and eaten. All Illini lived in fear. A plan was devised by a brave named Massatoga. He would stand and chant, acting as bait for the Piasa, while twenty of the bravest warriors hid in ambush. The scheme worked, and the Piasa was killed.

(drawing by Philip Hemstreet for the Institute of Fortean Studies)

Alton, llinois. This illustration of the Piasa graphically gives life to the rock painting record we have of this giant, winged beast. What was the relationship between these flying monsters and the Native Americans who had to live with them? Shaman and vision-seeking warriors are often mentioned in conjunction with the tales of the Piasa and other thunderbirds.

Among the Cherokee, the legend of the Tlanuwa is quite similar. On the north bank of the Little Tennessee River, in Blount County, Tennessee, is the cave of the Tlanuwa, immense birds who would fly up and down the valley. Often the giant beasts would come into villages and pick up dogs and even small children. Eventually a medicine man was approached and enlisted to rid the area of the Tlanuwa. He did, by killing the parent bird's young. Cherokee legend notes they were so furious they soared out of sight and were never seen again.

Or were they? When Amerindians living in the St. Louis-Alton area heard the white man's 1948 reports, they remembered the Piasa and other thunderbird accounts from their grandfathers and merely shook their heads.

Illinois' Big Birds of the 70s

The encounters with big birds in Illinois stretch through time from Marquette's notes of 1673 to the reports some three hundred years later. The 1977 incident detailed in *Mysterious America* of the two large birds swooping down and trying to pick up young Marlon Lowe was only the beginning of one of the biggest Thunderbird flaps to hit Illinois. And like others after them, all the 25 July witnesses—Mr. Cox, Jack and Betty Daniels, Jake, Marlon, Jackie and Ruth Lowe, and Mike Thompson—described exactly the same thing: two huge coal-black birds with long, white-ringed necks, long curled beaks, and wingspans of ten or more feet.

This Lawndale sighting was followed quickly by several others. On 28 July 1977 Stanley Thompson, his wife, and several friends saw one of the big birds fly over their farm late in the day. They were all watching some radio-controlled model airplanes when Mrs. Thompson said, "Look at that funny-looking plane that guy's flying." Soon she yelled, "It's a bird!", and everyone turned to watch. Stan told the sheriff's police the bird had a six-foot body and a wingspan of nine or ten feet. McLean County Sheriff's Sergeant Robert Boyd said Thompson "has been around here a long time. He's a credible witness. When I heard some of those earlier reports, I figured the people must be in the sauce. But these are responsible people. I've changed my mind, and we're going to investigate."

James Majors of Bloomington was the next witness. He was driving a mail truck from Armington to Delavan when he saw the birds. He said they had wingspans of over eight feet; plump bodies; straight tails; legs with claws for feet, about 2½ to 3½ feet long; pointed eight-inch-long bills; and mean/ugly-looking faces. He saw one glide into a nearby field and pick up a small animal, apparently a pig. Majors continued to drive into town, stopped, jumped out, and quickly smoked four cigarettes to regain his composure. "I think what I saw is a giant, large condor," Majors remarked soon after his late July sighting.

Late on Thursday, 28 July, Lisa Montgomery, eighteen, of Tremont was washing her car when she looked up and saw a giant bird with at least a seven-foot wingspan. "It was black, but I couldn't see its markings. It had a real low tail," she said. When it disappeared, it was flying toward Pekin, Illinois.

At 2:00 A.M. on Saturday, 30 July, Dennis Turner of Downs, Illinois and two of his friends saw a large bird with at least a six-foot wingspan perch on a telephone pole near the Gillum and Randolph Roads. Turner said the bird dropped something near the pole, and police later found a foot-long rat at the spot.

On the same day, Waynesville residents said they saw a large black bird with an eight-foot wingspan circling the area at about 2:00 P.M.

Texas John Affair

The 1977 flap of the Illinois big birds was filling the papers daily, and then the affair of "Texas John" occurred. On Saturday, 30 July, John Huffer of Tuscola, Illinois, and known locally as Texas John for reasons unknown, filmed what he says were the "big birds." Huffer, a sometimes-writer for *Bass Magazine*, construction worker, former Marine combat photographer, and an infrequent freelance television filmman, was out fishing with his son that hot July morning in 1977 when he saw the birds. Huffer said the two birds deposited baseball-sized droppings around a dead tree in which they had roosted. Huffer then scared them with his boat horn and commenced filming. After getting over one hundred feet of film of the two large birds, Huffer approached Champaign's WCIA-TV station and sold them part of the film for one newscast. He said the biggest bird's head was eighteen inches long, and its wingspan spread twelve feet.

Then things started getting a little bizarre. First there were the misquotes. For example, Huffer had observed, regarding the larger of the two birds: "I weigh 260 pounds, and I didn't want to get too close to it." By the time some wire services in this country and in England got the story, Huffer was quoted as saying the big bird had weighed 260 pounds!

Soon thereafter, Huffer, according to a statement he made to me in December of 1977, sold the description of the big bird, and "it is now (the) property of *Reader's Digest.*" He also was trying to make an arrangement with Sun Classic for the sale of his film. By February 1979 he was signing his letters "John Huffer The Native American Outdoor Writer" and asking for my assistance in disorganized letters. "*Help. Reader's Digest* is holding the real Big Bird story because I am an Indian," Huffer wrote. "We do not feel this is right. Please write to ...." The matter of Texas John or "Indian John" (as he was calling himself in 1979) distracted the press from the other straightforward reports of the big birds. By the time the Huffer story had hit the papers, the early Lowe/Lawndale abduction attempt was listed as "rumors and tales of birds kidnapping children." The press had found a way to start putting the lid on the stories, and Texas John was it.

The showing of the color film allowed the experts to quickly identify Huffer's birds as turkey vultures, and then label *all* the big birds seen as turkey vultures. Jack Ellis, Supervisor of Wildlife Resources for Illinois' Department of Conservation, issued a statement to the press that he had seen the film and the case was closed on all the nonsense about big birds. Dr. William K. Beecher, Director of the Chicago Academy of Sciences, said, "What we're seeing is a lot of hysteria, maybe some funning like the kangaroo stories we had a while back." (For detailed evidence that the Midwest's kangaroos are much more than some folks "funning" each other, see chapter 13: "Mystery Kangaroos" in *Mysterious America*. These phantom creatures have been seen throughout the U.S.A. since the 1800s by police officers, housewives, and scores of other credible witnesses.)

The whole Texas John affair is a strange one. If the attack by the experts on the big birds helped put into motion what we tend to call the "ridicule factor," the word must have not reached the birds. However, the end was in sight. Mrs. Albert Dunham, of rural Bloomington, was sitting in the second floor of her home about 4:00 P.M. on Sunday, 31 July, when she noticed a shadow passing outside over her house. At first she thought it was a cloud, but for some reason she glanced out and thought it was a small airplane. Then she took a good look and saw it was a big bird. "I've had my doubts about the reports, I really did," Mrs. Dunham said. "I wondered if I was just seeing something because of all the publicity." But she quickly realized something unusual was flying overhead. "It was twenty feet directly above me and I could pick out the underneath details very well. It was black with a white ring around its neck and white on its fan-like tail," she said. "It has a long straight bill and is a great big, huge bird." Her son chased it to a nearby landfill, but it vanished before a local newpaper's photographer could take a picture.

The Series Slows, the Experts and the Air Force

On Thursday, 11 August in southwestern Illinois, near Odin, the 1977 series of big bird sightings publicly ceased. John and Wanda Chappell were the last witnesses to come forward. They said they had seen a great, gray bird with a twelve-foot wingspan and six-foot-long body. "It was so big it had a hard time finding a limb big enough to land on," John Chappel remarked. His wife said, "It looked like a prehistoric bird. It was really fantastic. It was big enough to lift something. Our daughter is a year and a half old and it was big enough to lift a child bigger than her. It was that huge." In a hint of what people who were seeing the bird must have been feeling at this juncture of the flap, Wanda Chappell said, "We were hesitant to report it because we thought people might think we were exaggerating, but then I called my sister Alma. She said it was also sighted yesterday, so we thought if we reported it someone else might see it."

If it was seen again in Illinois in 1977, no one told the police or press. The notion the big birds were only turkey vultures, despite the fact turkey vultures have bright, distinctive red heads and a wingspan of less than six feet, was being widely reported in the papers. Why would witnesses dare have their names printed under headlines that read: "EXPERTS TALK TURKEY ON BIG BIRD STORY!?" The story was a dead one for the papers.

However, the big bird sightings continued, informally exchanged between local people interested in the subject. When I visited the Lowes in 1979, I was told of encounters that had occurred up to that time but were kept quiet for fear of more ridicule and harassment.

Illinois big bird stories are apparently even in the United States Air Force's UFO files. According to John Keel, Dr. Jacques Vallee, the famed French computer authority and ufologist who served as the model for the role played by Francois Truffaut in *Close Encounters of the Third Kind*, was given access to these files and found a curious big bird story. The report said an air force colonel was driving along an Illinois road one night (date not given) when he became aware of a huge bird the size of a small airplane directly overhead. It flapped its massive wings and soared away.

An Underlying Pattern?

Needless to say, the Illinois stories are not an isolated series of big bird encounters. Specific areas across the nation tend to have their histories of sightings. My files on the subject literally overflow. For example, the Black Forest region near Coudersport, Pennsylvania has a chain of incidents dating from the 1890s into the 1970s. I have articles and letters from folks in the Ozarks telling of thunderbirds carrying off kids and livestock from post-Civil War times until present. The series of New Jersey Devil accounts from the early 1900s and the Mothman sightings in Ohio and West Virginia in the 1960s both contain elements of the big birds' behavioral patterns, although both no doubt are admixtures of other cryptozoological and ufological items, as well. Since the *New York Times* story from 1937 of a Jarrett girl being lifted into the air by a huge bird to the 1976 accounts surveyed in my second book, *Creatures of the Outer Edge*, Texas has also had its big bird stories.

Making sense of this mass of tales, legends, sightings, and encounters is not an easy task. Amerindian folklore and backwoods knowledge appear to be the smoke above some interesting fires, but the lack of hard facts and details make it difficult to pin the stories on specific specimens of birds. The more recent accounts sometimes are misidentifications of known birds. I have not included all of the reports I have from very well-meaning people of the hawks, eagles, blue herons, or even peahens they have taken for something they weren't. Texas John Huffer's sighting over Lake Shelbyville, furthermore, could very well be a couple of turkey vultures. In any series of sightings, for example either the 1948 or 1977 Illinois accounts, I frequently am sorting through and discarding some sightings that are, no doubt, rare but common enough birds. And in the Illinois cases given in this chapter, I am positive a few of those stories are exaggerations of turkey vultures and other infrequent Illinois birds.

There remains, nevertheless, a hard core of sightings from Illinois and along the Ohio River Valley, from Appalachia and the Ozarks, from Utah, Nevada, California, Oklahoma, and Texas of large dark birds with wingspans of between ten and sixteen feet that carry off animals and attempt to abduct children.

Are Condors to Blame?

What could these birds be? They seem to have something to do with the largest known soaring birds presently accepted by ornithologists—the condors. So let's take a look at these birds. The Andean condor, *Vultur gryphus*, lives from seven thousand to sixteen thousand feet up in the Andes, from Columbia south to Tierra del Fuego. It is the world's largest flying bird, with a wingspan of about ten feet, which can reach twelve feet in some specimens. The Andean condor is glossy black with white upper-wing coverts, a bald head, and a white collar of feathers around its neck. They are known to attack and kill sick and small animals for food, although their primary source of meals is carrion, dead animals like deer, horses, sheep, and rabbits. Most bird experts state that the feet of this condor and its North American cousin are too weak to carry food for moderately far distances.

The California condor, *Gymnogyps californianus*, is smaller than the Andean condor. However, with a nine-foot wingspan, it is the largest flying bird in North America. The California condor is sooty black and lacks the white neck collar. (The 1977 series of Illinois big birds reportedly had white neck feathers, which would mean they were closer in appearance to the Andean condor than to the California.) The present range of the ten or so California condors (which obviously are close to extinction) is restricted to two counties in southern California, Santa Barbara and Ventura. Until recently, this condor lived throughout the extreme West, and in the early 1800s it lived in the East, according to Halliday's *Vanishing Birds*.

When California condors were more numerous they seemed to have moved around a lot more than they do now. In his 1958 book,

Extinct and Vanishing Birds of the World, James C. Greenway, Jr. observed: "In the past, a hundred and more years ago, there may have been a seasonal movement of population. This would account for the appearance of the birds near the Columbia River in Oregon in certain seasons." Greenway notes that there have been recorded "great congregations of birds in the autumn, particularly where food was plentiful."

Stepping back from the recent reports of big birds, a pattern of appearances does form. In late March, early April, and during July and August, from the Ozarks, down the Ohio River Valley, into the Appalachian Mountains, an irregular migration of the big birds appears to be occurring. The appearances in the western mountain states also seem to have a natural configuration to them.

Somewhat then, the appearance, behavior, flight patterns, and size of our big birds point to the condors being responsible for these recent reports. Is this possible? Are California condors, so low in numbers they are on the verge of extinction, flying about the Midwest scaring the daylights out of people? Are the big birds, then, condors? Probably not, I believe because: 1) of how closely the existing condors are watched; 2) the big birds are larger than the California condors; and 3) of the evidence that the big birds are so much more aggressive than are the condors.

But, I think a near relative of the condor is responsible. A relative that is still to be found in the wilderness craggies of the Bald Mountains that the Amerinds tell us are inhabited by thunderbirds and in the sheer cliff caves of the Smokies and Ozarks where backwoods people still tell of meetings with giant birds. Despite the interstates and jetports, those hilly outposts of nature do exist, and the big birds are calling them home.

The Terrible Teratorns

The candidate most in line with the big birds are the supposedly recently extinct teratorns. Feduccia in *The Age of Birds* sums them up this way:

> Perhaps the most remarkable of the Ice Age vulturine birds found in the New World were the teratorns. . . .The very common *Teratornis merriami* had a wing span of 11 to 12 feet, and *Teratornis incredibilis*, known from Pleistocene deposits in Nevada and

> California, had a wing span that may have approached 17 feet. But the real giant was an Argentine fossil. . . . nearly twice the size of *Teratornis merriami*, stood 5 feet tall and had a wing span of about 24 feet; it is the largest flying bird known to science.

Dr. Kenneth E. Campbell, one of the discoverers of the Argentine giant, has long studied the teratorns and disagrees with the usual assumption that they, like condors, were carrion-eaters. Campbell believes they were predators, based upon his investigation of *Teratornis merriami*, which are so numerous at the La Brea tar pits. "The long, narrow hooked beak and the type of mechanism found in this species are similar to those that grabbed small animals with its beak and swallowed them whole," Campbell has noted.

The bones of the teratorns have turned up in deposits from California to Florida, and it thus appears they were found throughout the United States of America, as well as the northern parts of Mexico. This distribution fits nicely with the reports of the big birds. Furthermore, the bones, some as recent as eight thousand years old, have almost always been found in conjunction with human habitation sites. Were the Amerindians killing these condor-like birds for their feathers or because the birds had been kidnapping their stock and children?

Did the teratorns look like our big birds? Interestingly, National Geographic and other official efforts to represent the teratorns have shown them as very condor-like with white ruffs around their neck, obviously modeling them after the Andean, not the California, condor. Still, as with all fossil remains, we really don't know what the teratorns looked like.

The long list of big bird sightings we have collected over the years may have to be reexamined someday by ornithologists. Right now, if you read their literature closely, you will find scholarly pieces on the possible "last sightings" of condors in Arizona's Yuma County in 1934 or a "questionable sighting recorded from Utah" in 1874. If a teratorn were caught in the near future, such a revelation may cause these same scientists to give some serious reconsideration to all the reports of big birds, from those such as the Logan County, Illinois ones to the account of a Piper Cub-sized bird viewed over Logan Street, Salt Lake City.

When that happens, I'll be glad to stop hearing about all those turkey vultures with twelve-foot wingspans.

4

THE JUNGLES
The Alux of the Yucatan

It was my way to note something, and not to regard it as isolated; and to search widely for other occurrences that might associate with it. — Charles Fort

February 1985, and my adventures were about to take me far from the cold temperatures of Maine to a warmer part of America where time has been somewhat forgotten, where the pace is low-key, and where the palm trees wave in the breeze of *El Norte*.

As the plane swept low over the massive expanse of closely knit hardwood trees, I was struck by how uninhabited this tourist mecca for oceanliners and diving enthusiasts really is. The tiny twenty-six-mile-long island of Cozumel was to be the jumping off point for my mini-expedition into the heart of the Yucatan, and I was surprised to find most of the island undeveloped outside of its small city of San Miguel. The Mexicana jet was banking now, and I had my first close look at the turquoise waters that beckon pleasure seekers from the United States of America to this other United States. Thoughts of the bejeweled temples of the Maya and the stories of unknown wonders raced through my head as the wheels of the 727 smoked upon touching the hot asphalt of the Mexican airport. Just a week before, according to Richard Greenwell, Secretary of the International Cryptozoology Society, someone had told him of filming a group of pterodactyls circling over the jungles of the Yucatan Peninsula. Naturally, as I was being transported to my intown hotel, images of *The Lost World* were in my mind as the taxi driver tried to avoid a four-foot iguana sunning itself calmly on the road. But I was not here primarily to track down stories of prehistoric flying reptiles; I was in pursuit of the tales of the little people, the *Alux* (ay-loosh). (Richard Heiden, archaeologist and Fortean, informs me the plural form may be "aluxob," but as "alux" is widely used for both the singular and plural forms, that is what I am employing.)

Americans and the Yucatan

But what am I doing in Mexico looking into more tales of mysterious America, you might ask? Then, first, please, a contextual note about this business of "Americans." Residents of the U.S.A. have a nasty habit of thinking of themselves as the only Americans around. Alan Riding's 1985 book, *Distant Neighbors: A Portrait of the Mexicans*, even notes it is downright disrespectful for the people north of the Rio Grande to always call themselves "Americans". Now, most tourist guidebooks for Mexico will correctly point out that U.S.A.ers and Canadians are more properly North Americans, and the rest of the folks in the so-called New World are either Central or Southern Americans. So for those people startled to find this chapter in a book whose core theme is the wonder of mysterious America, take heart in knowing I am extending the parameters of this tome to properly include the strange things experienced by our brothers and sisters throughout this hemisphere, Americans all.

From a zoogeographical point of view, however, there is a sharp break between north and south. The continental faunal regions, as named and bounded by Alfred Russell Wallace, neatly bissect Mexico, and that country has distinct animals that are said to live in either the Nearctic or the Neotropical Zones. Ivan T. Sanderson similarly divided the region along botanical lines, between what he calls the Erica and Columbia. Sanderson makes the point that within the area he calls the Columbia, the impact of mountains and fauna and flora are much more important as dividing lines than political borders. The literature on the Mexican peninsula of the Yucatan goes far to demonstrate this point to the extreme.

The Yucatan Peninsula, although part of the United States of

Mexico and lying north of Belize and Guatemala, is viewed as a separate entity unto itself, sticking out from the main body like a swollen knee. It is an isolated land, a giant plateau of limestone dotted with *cenotes*, huge holes filled with water. The vegetation is jungle-like, even technically a rain forest, according to the Smithsonian Institution's Professor Ayensu, but it is not the steamy jungle one imagines from Tarzan films. As Sanderson notes, the land "is clothed in an awful, low, tangled, spiny growth called *akalché*." These thorny bushes, stands of hardwood trees, and an occasional clump of palms and palmetto are hardly the stuff of the Amazon or the Congo, but such over- and undergrowth do keep the tourists away. In general, then, most human activity is limited to cleared spaces along the edges of this akalché, near roads or ports.

On to Quintana Roo

Leaving behind the skinny street dogs and dawn-crowing cocks of Cozumel, my colleagues (Libbet Cone, Lynn Bratman, and Richard Melito) and I took the ferry to the mainland. Our exploratory cryptozoological trip would quickly find us on the Yucatan proper, sleeping in a tent on the coast of Quintana Roo, near Punta Bete, at what is called a "camptel." Soon, we were able to hike about the area, collecting information on the seen and unseen world, and even occasionally finding ourselves in the midst of some akalché. During our time in Quintana Roo, we were able to see a large variety of wildlife common to the area and well-known to the native peoples thereabouts. These animals included everything from tarantulas to spider monkeys. On a quiet, hot afternoon's stroll down an unused road behind the camptel, we could easily disturb snake, coati, or iguana. Such visual sights were the rewards of the sweat beading on our brows.

Most North Americans coming to such spots as our camptel are mainly interested in enjoying the glorious nearby beach; not many realize the jungle a few paces away is teeming with life, both known and unknown. While anoles and opossums abound and are easily observed, the hidden life of the Yucatan is more difficult to comprehend. Rarely do visitors become aware that one of the most frequent accounts heard in the hinterland are those of the sightings of little people, modern day Yucatan pygmies.

The Archaeology of the Alux

Tales and rumors of these little people extend far back into the Yucatan's prehistory. At some Mayan temples there exist bas-reliefs of pairs of naked little men who are shown smaller than both the truly large priests and the five-foot tall Mayan Indian peasants represented in the carvings. The Mayas of today are still short people by Western standards, but these little people of the ancient petroglyphs were not Mayas and not children. They were fully grown peoples, shown amongst the legs of warriors and the like, carrying on adult activities. They were the Alux, a race of pygmies.

Anthropologists have been stumped by some of these carved figures. For example, at Seibal on the Pasion River, pictured on a number of stelae are strange people with long hair reaching all the way to their feet and possessing bone nose ornaments. T. Patrick Culbert, commenting in his book, *The Lost Civilization: The Story of the Classic Maya*, which is used by anthropology students worldwide, notes those "two features . . . distinguish this group of foreigners." Foreigners? From where, Culbert cannot say. "The newcomers may have been Maya—perhaps from some of the remote sections of the lowlands—but they certainly were not part of the Classic Maya Establishment," Culbert concludes.

In a related vein, travel writer Bill Mack and others have pointed out that at almost every Mayan archaeological site, one startling feature stands out. In front of the main temple usually are "either singly or in clusters . . . tiny 'houses' with doorways less than three feet high. Archaeologists write them off as 'votary shrines' but present-day Mayas say they were the homes of the favored Alux," according to Mack who has been on five major expeditions to the area. Rolf Schell, author of *A Yank in Yucatan*, photographed a group of these tiny huts at a secluded coastal site in the late 1950s. Asking his guide what they were, he was told "unequivocally" that the cluster was an Alux settlement.

Like Schell, I too was able to observe a possible Alux settlement in a good state of restoration. While in the Yucatan, I visited several major and minor Mayan ruins including the well-known sites of Chichen Itzá, Coba, and Tulum. One of the most enchanting places I explored was the Tulum site. Tulum is beautifully and dramatically set on a forty-foot sea cliff on the east coast of Quintana Roo. It has a wall on the land side, ten to eighteen feet high, twenty feet thick, with five gateways in its eight hundred yard length. Originally, a walkway topped the wall. (Other walled Mayan ruins include the archaeological areas of Mayapan, Xelhá, and Ichpaatun. The Alux may have an affinity for walled cities.)

Of the locations I visited, the strange small stone huts were most in evidence at the coastal ruin of Tulum. One cluster was especially prominent on a slight hill to the north of the main body of the temples. If the Alux did have a settlement at such places, as Mack and Schell would seem to indicate, they must have had a majestic view of the blue-green waters of the Caribbean. More importantly, of course, the Alux may have been involved somehow with local seatrading Mayas or with the Gulf Coast's Putun Mayas, who were early seafarers of the Caribbean.

Apes or Little People?

But the picture at Tulum is anything but clear. The involvement of the Alux here and at related sites is one explanation, but there are others. In 1842, when the great bushwhacker and explorer John L. Stephens found Tulum, he was told by local Mayas that the city had been built by strange apelike *corcubados*, or hunchbacks.

This confusion between two unknown forms, as in this case between anthropoid creatures and little people is nothing new in cryptozoology. I guess we should have been surprised if it did not turn up in the Yucatan. But besides this business of the "hunchbacks" of Tulum we have, via Bernard Heuvelmans, this curious document cited by Professor Georges Montandon as having come from the *Science News Letter* of the 1920s:

> Monstrous stone statues like gorillas, coming from the gorilla-less country of the Mayas, are one of the unexplained curiosities of the archaeological and historical Museum of Merida (Yucatan). There are two of these creatures without legs, but standing upright more than five feet high on the stumps of their thighs . . . they were found near the town of Tekax in Yucatan . . . . The figures have a strikingly apelike position. They have pronounced eyebrows, broad chests and a bent back. There is no trace of any legend which explains their significance, and the inhabitants of Tekax know only that these stone statues have been for a long time in their lonely position on the hill.

Professor Montandon commented at the time, however, that the local Indians said pygmies still lived in the Motilone area. Montandon then made the jump to assuming the "little men" reported by the Mayas might be large apes as portrayed in the Tekax "gorilla" statues. For my own part, I do find it interesting that the Tekax beings are represented as having "bent backs," which may relate to the tales of the Tulum "hunchbacks." Whether or not they are "gorillas" or some as yet undiscovered New World ape is another matter altogether.

And Giants Too?

Besides the ape/little people complexities, there are the mainly Mexican and Guatemalan stories of *El Sisimite*. Usually the sisimite is represented as a giant, but here again, there's some confusion about some of the stories. Let's look at this sisimite business.

Ivan T. Sanderson in his classic book, *Abominable Snowmen: Legend Come to Life*, concentrates, through several pages of discussion, on the sisimite. One of the earliest mentions of the sisimite found by Sanderson was in the University of Pennsylvania Museum's *The Museum Journal*, volume VI, number 3, September 1915. The article shows that the sisimite, or sisimici "is a monster that lives in the forest. He is taller than the tallest man, and in appearance he is between a man and a monkey." According to the article, numerous stories are told of local people being kidnapped by the sisimite. The piece then goes on to tell of one such incident that happened near Mount Kacharul in Guatemala.

Sanderson noted *The Museum Journal*'s story of a woman captured by a sisimite was almost identical to one he had collected from the early 1940s from a Coban (Guatemala) police blotter. The report stated a sisimite had entered Miguel Huzul's son-in-law's house, and in the presence of other witnesses had taken away Huzul's daughter. The son-in-law had just sat there shivering, a common reaction in such cases, apparently, as it was mentioned in the journal article also, and labeled "sisimite shivers." The police did not know quite what to make of the report, jotted it down as a creature of the mountains like "a sort of gorilla or man," and apparently tried to forget it as quickly as possible. Sanderson quipped: "I presume there is no precise law covering such matters."

Another examination concerns Sanderson's associates, Cal Brown and Wendell Skousen, and their inquiries in an area around the town of Cubulco, in Baja Verapaz, Guatemala. This location is in the Sierra de Chuacus range of mountains, whose highest peak is Mt. (Cerro) Sanché, at eighty-five hundred feet elevation. In Skousen's words:

> There live in the mountain forests very big, wild men, completely clothed in short, thick, brown, hairy fur, with no necks, small eyes, long arms and huge hands. They leave footprints twice the length of a man's . . . . Sometimes (it) walked on two legs, and apparently ran on all fours . . . . It looked like a bear, but it *wasn't* from the description . . . (the locals) gave—no conspicuous ears, no "snout"—it was somewhat taller than a man, and considerably broader, covered with darkish hair . . . . Several people reported they were chased by it down the mountain.

In Richard Oglesby Marsh's *White Indians of Darien*, published in 1934, reference is made to a Mr. Shea who claimed he killed a huge apeman in Panama.

The *Bulletin of the United States Bureau of American Ethnology* of 1932 also discusses the "sisimite" in its survey of the Indians of Honduras and Nicaragua. On unexplored mountains in the region are said to be tailless anthropoid apes, the sisimites, of erect position, about five feet tall and covered with black hair. Apparently they are greatly feared for they are supposed to carry off human beings of the opposite sex. The journal article concludes by noting: "Some Indians claim that this mysterious being has been seen several times during the last twenty years around the Guarunta Mountains, which extend northward of the lower Rio Coo."

Charles Wisdom, writing in 1940 in *The Chorti Indians of Guatemala*, notes the Chorti had many encounters with the hairy sisimites who were reported to have stolen children and kidnap adults if alone, the male carrying off women and the female, men. They are believed to throw stones down the side of mountains at night. The sisimite live on uninhabited hills and near secluded streams far from human habitations.

From these tales of the sisimite, the beasts sound like a form of Central American Bigfoot, leaving huge footprints, kidnapping young maidens, and generally being large and hairy. But are the sisimite so easy to catalog? In 1963 and 1964, I exchanged letters with Carlos Eduardo Cardona, Secretariá del Estado Mayor del Jefe de Gobierno, of Guatemala City. Although discounting the tales as myths, Cardona clearly informed me the stories he had gathered and the news reports he had read about the "sisimite" indicated they were "small people" who walked about at night, usually alone. And Bill Mack in his article on the little people of the Yucatan noted one name used for them is "Sisimite."

Back to the Alux

Whatever the origin of the sisimite stories, whether giants or little people, returning to the Yucatan and nearby Belize, we are on firmer ground relating the Alux stories to little people, and not to apes or to Bigfeet. For example, a 1944 Belize newspaper account tells of a government timberman's encounter with two small people deep in the British Honduras hardwood jungles.

And from 1977, we have the sterling report of a young Mayan named Xuc (pronounced "Chuck"). Xuc was at the time the caretaker of the archaeological site of Mayapan, an ancient walled Mayan city that became the capital after the fall of Chichen Itzá. Bill Mack, in his excellent article, "Mexico's Little People," in the August 1984 issue of *Fate,* tells of Xuc's meeting with an Alux:

> Mayapan ... is closed to visitors after 5:00 P.M. and therefore ... Xuc was puzzled late one night in 1977 to hear the sound of a machete chopping wood. Unlocking the entry gate, he started in the direction of the sound. As he rounded the corner of the dilapidated Temple of the Birds, a small clay pellet whizzed perilously close to his head. He ducked behind a pile of fallen masonry and heard pellet after pellet strike the ancient stones around him.
>
> During a pause in this strange barrage, Xuc raised his head and peered out cautiously. What he saw shook him to the foundations of his traditional Indian stoicism. Outlined in the wavering moonlight was a tiny man. His head was disproportionately large, his beard was jet-black and he was clad in a white *hupile,* a Mayan dress-like garment or tunic. Slung over his shoulder was a standard-sized machete almost as long as the man was tall.
>
> What Xuc saw was living proof—for him at least—that the Alux exist.

When Bill Mack interviewed Xuc late in the 1970s, he found the young man bright, personable, and well-educated. Still, Mack had problems with the disturbing story the man had to tell. Xuc, sensing disbelief in the North American's questions, left his hut and returned soon with a small cloth sack. In it were about eight clay pellets the size of walnuts, Mack tells us in his article. He felt they had been carefully made and baked to "bulletlike" hardness. These pellets were the ones Xuc had found the day after his encounter with the Alux.

Central and South American Little People

Bill Mack, Ivan Sanderson, Bernard Heuvelmans, and others have observed that the little people stories such as those about the Alux are found from the Yucatan Peninsula, down through the rain forests of Central and South America, all the way to Tierra del Fuego. Whether labeled Alux, Toyo, or one of the other variants, the local residents appear to be describing humanoid beings smaller than the five-foot-tall Mayas. The trail of the pygmies runs for hundreds of miles, through many countries, languages, and cultural groups. (Whether the tales of the sisimite or Tulum's corcubados are part of the little people tradition gone astray will have to remain an open question for now.)

In Belize, the Coast Caribs and residents of Western extraction tell of small human-like creatures living in their southern jungle. They are called *Dwendis*, a corruption of *Duende*, Spanish for goblin. About forty years ago, a forestry officer saw two of these creatures near the foot of the Maya Mountains, in what was then British Honduras. They were three and a half to four and a half feet tall, and covered in thick, brown fur with flat yellowish faces. The footprints of the Dwendis are said to show very pronounced pointed heels.

In Guatemala, anthropologist Charles Wisdom collected many stories of the *Duende*, dwarves which dwelled in the hills and valleys, he was told. These little people are especially fond of living close to groups of cattle and stealing children.

In Ecuador, the four-to-five-foot creatures are called *Shiru* and described as hominoid, but are fully covered in short, dark brown hair. In the mountain forests of the Guiana Highlands of Brazil, French Guiana, Suriname, Guyana, and Venezuela, the Arawaks, Caribs, and other native South Americans refer to their little creatures as *Didi, Dru-di-di, Didi-aguiri*, or some other related form. The Indians say they are short, strong, and hair-covered.

British Guiana, now Guyana, has had a long history of contact between the *Didi* and English residents. During their "discovery" of the country in 1596 and 1597, Sir Walter Raleigh and Laurence Keymis heard rumors of creatures resembling fauns and satyrs of the Old World. In 1769, Dr. Edward Bancroft chronicled stories of what he assumed was a large ape. Bancroft wrote that it was "represented by the Indians as being near five feet in height, maintaining an erect position, and having a human form, thinly covered with short black hair." Bancroft felt the height was exaggerated by fear.

(Edward Bancroft, internationally known as an expert on tropical plants, is an interesting figure in cryptopolitical history, as well. Benjamin Franklin had sponsored Bancroft for membership in the Royal Society of London. When Franklin was at the American Embassy in Paris, Edward Bancroft, Franklin's friend and chief assistant, organized a cell of British spies, beginning in 1772. During his sojourn in Paris, Bancroft left weekly dispatches for the British written in invisible ink between the lines of love letters of a "Mr. Richardson" and placed in a bottle in a hollow tree at the Tuileries. Franklin, who was involved in occult circles, such as the Lodge of the Nine Sisters in Paris and Sir Francis Dashwood's Hell-Fire Club outside of London, is viewed by Richard Deacon in his *A History of British Secret Service* as merely part of the British intelligence network set up by Bancroft and others.)

The encounters have continued through the years. Foremost among them, perhaps, is the 1910 meeting between the British Resident Magistrate, Mr. Haines and a couple of Didi. Magistrate Haines had come upon the small, reddish brown fur-covered creatures while he was prospecting for gold along the Konowaruk, just above the junction with the Potaro River. He said they had slowly retreated into the forest without once taking their eyes off him.

Discoveries of My Trek

With this background of reports and folklore in my head, my journey to the Yucatan naturally was directed towards discovering if the little-people tradition was still alive and whether current accounts existed. Certainly the anecdotal evidence for pygmies appears to exist in a concentrated fashion from the Guianas up through the Yucatan, and thus I was excited to get a chance to talk to some local Mayan people about the stories of the Alux.

While staying at the camptel, I soon got some assistance from an intelligent, personable, and pulchritudinous woman from Colorado, Amy Cole. As the person in charge of managing the Mayan staff who maintained and cooked for the camptel, Cole had daily contact with the Mayas. Her grasp of Spanish was excellent, and she was highly respected by the Mayas for her ability to learn their language. Amy Cole served ably as my translator in my quest for the latest on the Alux.

Cole soon discovered for me that the boss of the Mayan crew, Herman, a down-to-earth, no-nonsense sort of fellow, had experienced a close encounter with the Alux. Herman's episode had centered on his family farm, his *milpa*. Only a few miles from Playa de Carmen in Quintana Roo, Herman often went back and forth between the camptel and his milpa. A couple of years ago, Herman had returned to his milpa and became violently ill. He immediately felt the Alux were around. Going to his melon patch, which he had only recently checked, he found seventy watermelons had been destroyed. Soon after he arrived and found the ruined crop, Herman was hit by what he decribed as many small "stone-like objects." Although he could not see who or what was hurling the objects at him, he knew their source from the traditions of his people. Making a hasty retreat, Herman knew he was under attack by the Alux.

Herman stated over and over again that it was significant that these things thrown at him were "stone-like," and not natural rocks, pebbles, or stones. Needless to say, when we collected this account and compared it to the accounts detailing the so-called "sisimite shivers" and to Xuc's Mayapan report of the clay pellets, we too found it quite significant. (For the record, I would like to note that this business of these thrown "manufactured" pellets is rather disturbing if we are to view these accounts on a purely cryptozoological plane. However, the poltergeist literature is filled with reports of stones and stone-like objects floating, falling, and otherwise being cast at people worldwide. As Charles Fort noted, the simplest form of teleportation is the slow flows of stones into open fields. Whether or not these Alux pellets fit into the context of apported or teleported objects is an unanswered question.)

Herman, although never having seen the Alux himself, knew from other Mayas that the Alux are short, small, and yet very powerful people. Although the Alux are found all over the Yucatan, Herman had heard they are especially active in the mountains around Chemax, near the ancient Mayan capital of Chichen Itzá. They are known to guard money and treasures found in caves and cenotes. And in an interesting detail not found in any of the other accounts I have seen, Herman calmly stated that the female Alux are very beautiful and have very large breasts.

None of the other Mayas I was able to speak with, via Amy Cole, had been as close to an Alux as Herman, but the Alux are well-known, nevertheless. The Mayas from villages, such as Herman's, tended to be closer to the first-hand accounts of the Alux and viewed them as very real little people. The so-called Mexicanized Mayas living and working in towns like Playa de Carmen often laughed off the Alux as something like fairy stories or elf tales. That is until you sat with them for awhile, and they learned you were a North American who wanted to hear what they really knew and felt about the Alux and not what they had censored for their Mexican employers, neighbors, or friends. Often, after some soothing *té caliente* the city Mayas would tell, straight-faced and seriously, about how small, childlike footprints had been found several times across a certain Playa hotel's newly mopped kitchen floor, and only the Alux could be to blame as the local children had been all accounted for.

After several days amongst the iguanas, palm trees, and sunshine of the Yucatan, I came away certain the Mayas are still encountering small pygmies in the jungles of the area. But as Herman told me, nothing in the world would convince him to help anyone go look for them. The elusive Alux will have to remain, for now, hidden in the tall, wet hardwoods and short, dry, thorned akalché of the Yucatan.

And, Oh Yes, The Pterodactyls of the Yucatan?

What evidence did we find of the pterodactyls? Well, if a bonafide film shows up, I certainly will be happy to be the first to view it and dig into its origins, but after my trip to the area, I came away with some possible conventional explanations for what the man had filmed. First, the circling birds found most often throughout the Yucatan are vultures, and some drift so high, one might lose all sense of their avian affinities. Another large bird, which likewise also floats and soars high into the sky, especially along the coastal jungle sections, is the Magnificent Frigatebirds, formerly called Man-o'-War Birds (*Fregata magnificens*). These seabirds have wingspans measuring seven and a half feet across, and the sharp angular bends of the wings certainly made the ones I saw look prehistoric and reptilian.

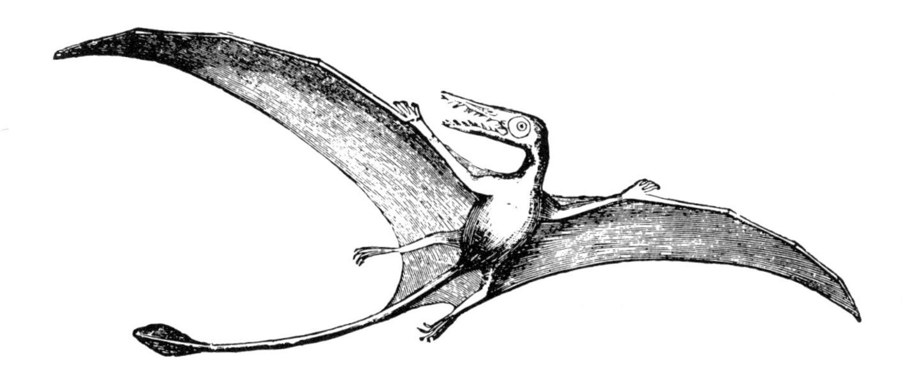

(courtesy of the Institute of Fortean Studies)

Yucatan Peninsula, United States of Mexico. Is there any basis to the recent reports of pterodactyls from the jungles of the little explored Yucatan?

Or maybe the man had filmed an as yet undiscoverd fruit bat of the Yucatan? (See my *Creatures of the Outer Edge*, for a discussion of unknown giant bats seen along the Rio Grande, near Brownsville, Texas and Ivan Sanderson's *Investigating the Unexplained* for some similar accounts from Africa and the Orient.)

The final word on the pterodactyls of Quintana Roo, however, may have come from Herman, the man who had told me so much about the Alux. Showing Herman a museum representation of a pterdodactyl, which I had brought along on this mini-expedition for just such identification purposes, I asked him what, in his language, would his villagers call this thing? Wondering if Herman might regale me with stories of hilltop-lost worlds and dinosaurs, I was struck silent by his answer. Amy Cole, translating once again, nonplused, told me, "Oh, he says, they would call that an eagle."

Little people, *sí*. Pterodactyls, *no!*

5

THE CITIES
Urban Jungle Beasties

We have had some experience with conclusions that were said to be obvious. —Charles Fort

Of course, it never ceases to amaze people somewhat unfamiliar with the sightings I investigate, that yes, these things are happening all the time and sometimes in *their* neighborhoods. Folks assume that the creatures and things that go bump in the night are being seen only in some god-forsaken rural setting and never would dare show themselves in crowded suburban and urban surroundings. The cases, however, prove something else altogether.

Monkeyman

During the first week in October 1982, reports out of Hoboken, New Jersey told of an ape-like creature quickly labeled "Monkeyman." Unlike the locale for the Bigfoot accounts from the Pacific Northwest, Hoboken is not a heavily forested wilderness area. Instead it is a one-square-mile community of forty-three thousand people situated on the Hudson River, not far from New York City. "Seems that a fellow who hadn't been shaving much lately was spotted hanging around a Hoboken playground," noted the *New York Post*. The stories about the thing developed to the point, the paper went on, so:

"within days, mysterious hunchbacked Monkeyman—half ape, half human, all rumor—was terrorizing school hallways, throwing students out of windows, and killing a teacher."

The explosive nature of the tales surprised school officials and police authorities. Soon the "wipe" (a special Fortean term related to newspaper and official attempts to bury a story) was in full force. Public Safety Director, James Giordano, flatly told the press: "There is no Monkeyman, no students missing, no children missing. We went looking for him—he wasn't even in the streets. But how do you stop a rumor that's spreading like wildfire?" Detective Commander Patrick Donatacci continued this line of thinking in his comments. "It's just a vicious rumor that got out of hand. It's a strange thing—once they hear something, they don't believe the truth when they hear it. They'd rather believe fiction."

On Friday, 15 October the local authorities were still so upset by the Monkeyman accounts they formed a task force to enlighten all the teachers and school principals as to the true facts or nonfacts behind the case. As the *New York Post* cleverly put it: "In an effort to kill a monster that never existed, cops in Hoboken, N.J. are spreading the word around grade school that Monkeyman is a lot of monkey business." Safety Director Giordano's three officer Juvenile Aid Bureau were given a task they probably never could have imagined they would be assigned, namely to wipe out an entity entitled Monkeyman.

We get a slight chuckle from the apparent mischief caused by this supposed nonentity. For something that did not exist, Monkeyman certainly stirred up lots of people. We are reminded of the old ufological view of the world, that, for heaven's sakes, it does not matter whether there are flying saucers or not, for the *impact* they have had on us is so great that their existence is hardly important any longer. So be it with Monkeyman.

Some mighty bizarre and therefore unforgettable creatures have been encountered in the last two decades in the concrete morass of America.

St. Louis' Thing

In 1963, from about 9 May until the twenty-third, St. Louis, Missouri and Centerville, Illinois were engulfed in flap after flap of strange monster stories.

Several youngsters reported a "half man, half woman with a half bald head and a half head of hair." Now, you must remember this was long before the days of Boy George and punk rock, so the kids were rather startled by this character. The thing was said to be a sometime resident of the Ninth Street housing project and would disappear into an old subway on Twelfth Street. Sounding more like one of Ray Palmer's "deros" from the hollow Earth than a cryptozoological specimen, this St. Louis "thing" was taken seriously by the police.

I investigated the case at the time and discovered the police were saying some rather interesting things. "Those kids were sincere. They saw something," noted Patrolman Bill Conreux of the St. Louis Police Department. "Supposedly it scuffled with a man near the Patrick Henry School."

Soon thereafter, on 18 May, Centerville, Illinois, just across the Mississippi River from St. Louis, was visited by a bizarre denizen of the unknown. When I shared my report on this case with John Green, famed Canadian Sasquatch researcher, he was shocked to hear that the police in Centerville had received over fifty calls in one night about this beast. One man, James McKinney, said the monster, which he described as a half man/half horse, was right in front of his house. The police never caught up with this thing, and by the twenty-third of that crazy month in 1963, they were only getting three calls a night.

Giant Cats of the City

If a Monkeyman in Hoboken and Centaurs in the St. Louis area were not enough, than a lion loose in the U.S.A. capital might convince you that some strange inhabitants of the urban jungle are trying to make themselves known.

On 10 August 1982 uniformed Secret Service officer Leonard G. Gooch spied a mysterious feline "about half the size of a full grown lion" scurrying between the stately mansions along Massachusetts Avenue N.W. and disappearing behind the Iranian Embassy. Over fifty law enforcement officers, National Zoo vets, and other official searchers did some intensive looking but did not find any big cats. Yes, one "gray, fox-sized" animal was flushed out of the nearby bushes, and humorous news accounts tried to quip that the beast might turn out to be a field mouse. However, with a police helicopter hovering overhead as this District of Columbia lion disappeared into the annals of urban phantom critters, we must guess the answers hardly lie in the realm of mice.

The reports of urban phantom felines continue to roll in. During the end of May 1984, a huge black panther was seen prowling the residential streets of Manchester, Michigan. A few days later, on 1 June, one was spied on Long Island, New York, near exit 70 of the expressway. A sighting of an African lion occurred in the Cleveland, Ohio suburb of North Olmsted in July 1984. The following month, at least five sightings of a black panther took place near the Fisher Body Plant in Flint, Michigan. This cat made some return appearances in December 1984, as did a large feline variously described as like a mountain lion, a roaring lion, or a Bengal tiger to the Cincinnati, Ohio suburb of North Avondale.

(courtesy of Ray Boeche)

Urban America. Giant black phantom panthers and maned mystery lions have recently and increasingly been reported in the concrete jungles of the cities. Formerly they were more frequently seen in rural locations in North America, but the appearance of urban apemen, centaurs, sewer gators, mystery kangaroos, phantom pachyderms, and the ghostly felines appear to demonstrate a spread of the strange creatures beyond their old haunts.

Finally, Fort Worth, Texas was visited by a maned mystery cat during February 1985. It began on Wednesday, 20 February at about 7:45 P.M., when Michael Tracy, thirty-seven, and a friend were sitting in Tracy's van near the Fort Worth Zoo. They were trying to relax, enjoying a quick meal on their dinner break from work, when suddenly they heard a roar. Being so close to the zoo, they did not think much of it at first, but the roaring continued, and it sounded mighty close. "It was a lion, no doubt about it." Tracy said right after his encounter. "I shined my light on it, and he was big, and he was mad about something."

Tracy rushed to a convenience store and called police. Escorted back to the scene by six police cars, Tracy's lion was soon seen by two police officers. Patrolman S.D. Roberts swears what he saw that night at about 9:45 P.M. was a lion too. "I had my spotlight out, and I saw something moving. I caught a silhouette from the side. It had the shape of a lion's head. It moved like a large cat, and it had a long tail. He turned and looked at us, and it was a big, big cat. His eyes were set wide apart," Roberts said. "I've been to the zoo, and I know what an African lion looks like." Like Tracy, the officers noticed it had a mane. Police searched the area on foot, by searchlights, and with a helicopter, but came up empty-handed. And yes, the zoo was checked, and no big cats were missing. Elvie Turner, the zoo's director, commented that if it was a lion on the loose, it would have a big appetite. "The first thing I checked was the zebras," he said.

After searchers found nothing, the next morning various authorities started coming up with explanations. One that was especially favored said the lion was a trained Britanny spaniel. That just didn't set right with the policemen who had actually seen the beast. "This wasn't a bird dog," said Officer D.W. Gill. "I grew up with bird dogs."

But after a few days of warning joggers not to run in that part of the city and keeping the kids in from recess at the nearby Lily B. Clayton Elementary School, things returned to normal. Or as normal as they can get after a city has had such a curious encounter of the phantom feline kind.

And Kangaroos Too

The notorious mystery kangaroos (see *Mysterious America*, chapter 13) have also of late been invading the cities. On Sunday, 23 September 1984 a woman motorist reported to the authorities she had seen a kangaroo hop across I-94 at the Detroit, Michigan Metropolitan Airport. The next morning sheriff's deputies reported the same thing. Kangaroos, of course, are from Australia, not Michigan. But as in the scores of such cases like those that I have examined, nothing was ever caught, and no one came up with a "logical" explanation for this creature from nowhere.

Sewer Gators: And Now the Coverup

Speaking of solving urban mysteries, none is more challenged by officialdom and the *New York Times* as the story of the alligators-in-the-sewers. Frequent stories appear debunking the existence of actual cases of alligators being found in the New York sewers, as I documented in *Mysterious America*. However, what is interesting is some of the stories we are beginning to hear about this whole affair and from some rather impressive places.

Recently, for example, New York attorney Ronald Rosenblatt wrote me of an unusual exchange he had concerning the matter at hand. I'll let Rosenblatt tell the story:

> The incident occurred in 1979, when I went on a guided tour of Pelham Bay Park in the Bronx. The tour was led by two Urban Park Rangers, who are headquartered at The Dairy in Central Park.
>
> One of the two Urban Park Rangers was named Pat Faiella. He told me he had studied Natural Sciences at St. Francis college. In the course of our walk, we had a long conversation and had an interesting discussion about urban wildlife.
>
> We started talking about alligators in the sewers and I asked Faiella if he took the subject seriously. He said that he did and that he had seen a museum maintained by the New York City Sanitation Department where stuffed specimens and photographs of alligators and crocodiles from the New York sewers were on display.

Rosenblatt thought the story was "odd" at the time, but did not think the Ranger was "putting him on." Instead, Rosenblatt found Faiella to be intelligent and serious.

My attempts to track Faiella have been frustrated by his leaving the service of the city, and his supervisor at the time, Steve

Young, does not know where to locate him. Young, also, has no knowledge of sewer gators.

New York City denies they have a museum, but if Rosenblatt is right, out on Randall's or Ward's Island, there may exist one of the strangest exhibits ever assembled by city employees. As we know, alligators were poisoned and shot in the sewers of New York in the 1930s, according to that era's Superintendent May, and perhaps some stuffed specimens were preserved and still do exist.

Until New York City debunks its debunkers, the coverup continues.

A Highrise Elephant

Elusive and uncatchable, mystery airport kangaroos, crazy sewer crocs, and phantom suburban felines may still sit nicely in the files of creature chroniclers—although the new aggressive moves into the cities are somewhat disturbing. But how in the world are we to assess rumors, sightings, and bureaucratic search parties for an urban pachyderm?

Maybe there are more reports of them out there. Maybe not. But the one from 2 May 1979 is upsetting enough. Sightings on that date were reported of a little elephant near a warehouse in the Bay Ridge section of Brooklyn, New York City. Bay Ridge's claim to fame is the movie *Saturday Night Fever*, so an elephant certainly seemed an unusual enough way for that section of New York to get a little publicity. But the authorities took the reports seriously. The classic search party—individuals from the Bureau of Animal Affairs, City Health Department, and the American Society for the Prevention of Cruelty to Animals—looked and questioned and looked and queried, all to no avail. Local television station, Channel 5, sent up a helicopter, another part of the classic safari syndrome, and as usual found nothing.

At one point, Dr. Howard Levin of New York City's Bureau of Animal Affairs may have thought he was pretty close to getting his phantom pachyderm. Approaching one Bay Ridge resident, Dr. Levin asked: "Have you ever seen an elephant about the neighborhood?"

After solemn consideration, the man replied: "What kind?"

6

THE SWAMPS
Creatures from the Black Lagoon

The trouble in trying to understand all reported monsters is their mysterious appearances and disappearances. —Charles Fort

In John A. Keel's *Strange Creatures from Time and Space*, chapter 10 is devoted entirely to a hodgepodge of mostly American beasts Keel felt in some way were related to the Abominable Snowman and Bigfeet. These ape-like monsters, said to be roaming the "hollers and hills" of the eastern and southern United States, have always been a focus of my research efforts, and one third of Keel's cases for his chapter came from my files. I wondered, however, what it was about Keel's grouping that made me feel uncomfortable. Finally, it dawned on me that Keel had labeled the chapter somewhat inappropriately. His title, "Creatures from the Black Lagoon," was a very catchy Keelian way of noting something strange was slithering through the swamps, but the original movie monster he had used as the model was anything but ape-like. The eponymous *Creature from the Black Lagoon* was a reptilian "gillman," a bipedal, human-sized beast that looked more like a spiny skinned were-lizard than a hairy were-gorilla or werewolf. The thing was literally a half-man, half-amphibious reptile.

Now, as creatures go, these types of monsters are rare, but by no means nonexistent. A lot of monster lumping does occur by Forteans and cryptozoologists, so my task was to closely examine the accounts of existing swamp creatures, be they termed Bigfoot, river monsters, or whatever, to reveal the true Creatures from the Black Lagoon.

West Coast Cases

One classic Bigfoot story, (discussed in some detail in *Mysterious America*) namely, the Wetzel/Riverside, California sighting on 8 November 1958, clearly fits the reptilian mode better than the anthropoid one. Wetzel described, as you may recall, the fluorescent-eyed "thing" as having a protuberant mouth and a body covered with scales, looking like leaves. Wetzel's "thing" emerged from the Santa Ana River underbrush.

The connection to water is a strong theme in all of these accounts so it is not so surprising that the next piece of the puzzle comes from the lake monster file. Trekking up the West Coast, the following report concerns a monster that actually looks like it stepped out of the wardrobe room of the Black Lagoon movie.

Thetis Lake is near Colwood, British Columbia, not far from Victoria. Cadboro Bay, off Victoria and Vancouver Island, is well known for the perennial sea monster "Cadborosaurus," so understandably a new creature in the neighborhood would be grouped under the same type of facade by the press. But the Thetis Lake Monster appears to be something else altogether.

On 19 August 1972 Gordon Pike and Robin Flewellyn said a five-foot-tall animal appeared on the surface of Thetis Lake and chased them from the beach. Flewellyn was cut on the hand by six razor-sharp points atop the monster's head. A Royal Canadian Mounted Police officer was quoted at the time as saying: "The boys seem sincere, and until we determine otherwise we have no alternative but to continue our investigation."

The next Wednesday afternoon, 23 August, the Thetis Monster was encountered again. Mike Gold and Russell Van Nice said they saw "it" around 3:30 P.M. and on the other side of the lake away from the recreation area of its first appearance. Mike Gold noted: "It came out of the water and looked around. Then it went back in the water. Then we ran!" He described the creature as "shaped like an ordinary body, like a human being body but it had a monster face, and it was all scaly . . . (with) a point sticking out its head (and) great big ears." It was silver.

At last word, the RCMP were investigating the Thetis Monster "because it's been reported to us, and we have to check these things out."

(Puget Sound, in Washington is equally as rich. The Kwakiutl Indian merman, Pugwis, is sort of a cross between Sasquatch and the Creature from the Black Lagoon. Fish-like face and paired incisors make this undersea spirit a prominent figure in Indian legend and easily recognized in wood-carved art.)

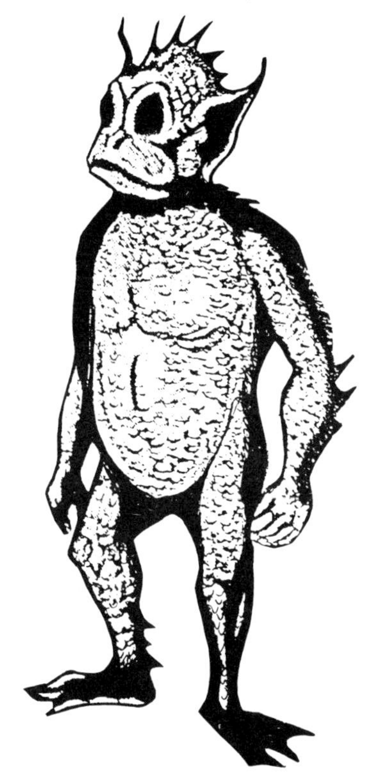

(courtesy of the Institute of Fortean Studies)

Thetis Lake, British Columbia. Over a period of three days in 1972, this monster scared the daylights out of residents of the area. This drawing based on witnesses' descriptions shows the humanoid and gillman features of this bizarre Creature from the Black Lagoon.

On To the Great Lakes

The Thetis Monster account sounds similar to one from Saginaw, Michigan, occurring in 1937. A man-like monster climbed up a river bank, leaned against a tree, and then returned to the river. The fisherman who witnessed this appearance suffered a nervous breakdown. This Saginaw tale, the reports of clawed and three-toed prints from Wisconsin to Missouri, and other supposedly "Bigfoot" or "manimal" encounters perhaps should be reexamined in light of the reptilian Creatures from the Black Lagoon.

The big Deltox Swamp, Wisconsin flap, investigated by Ivan T. Sanderson in 1969, for example, has always been shelved with Bigfoot reports. But what is to be made of the tracks of the creature, like footprints of "a good-sized man with swim fins."

This trait is a more frequent characteristic in the so-called eastern Bigfoot reports than you might realize. For example, there's the case of the creature of Charles Mill Lake in Mansfield, Ohio. A green-eyed, seven-foot tall, seemingly armless humanoid, seen late in March, 1959 by Michael Lane, Wayne Armstrong, and Dennis Patterson, came out of the lake and left behind "tracks that resembled the footgear worn by skin divers." The thing was seen again in 1963 and described as "luminous and green-eyed." I examined the site of these encounters and can testify to the Charles Mill Lake's swampy affinities certainly a good home for a Black Lagoon beast.

In the annals of midwestern monster hunters is a cryptic chapter few discuss as they talk about the fieldwork done at Louisiana, Missouri. In the early 1970s, many folks looked into the widespread reports of "Momo" (Missouri Monster). One investigator was traveling down a back road and was surprised to see what *appeared* to be a grown man dressed in complete skin diving gear down to the swimfins, miles from a logical skindiving site. Does this report of a "frogman" have something to do with our inquiry?

The quest is pulling us to the Midwest, U.S.A. and is taking an even more unorthodox view of some already weird wonders. But before we get caught up in the focus of the accounts, let's deal with matters in New Jersey and New York.

Mid-Atlantic Swamps

In a continuous watery line down the Susquehanna River through the so-called Southern Tier of New York State, into the Tamarack swamps along the Delaware ending in the counties of Morris and Sussex, New Jersey, reports, tales, and sightings of Creatures from the Black Lagoon are a matter-of-fact. In 1973, during the summer, residents of New Jersey's Newton-Lafayette area described a giant, man-like alligator they had seen locally. Newspaper reporters wrote about an old Indian tale from the region that told of a giant, man-sized fish that could never be caught. In 1977, New York State Conservation Naturalist Alfred Hulstruck reported that the state's Southern Tier had "a scaled, man-like creature (that) appears at dusk from the red, algae-ridden waters to forage among the fern and moss-covered uplands."

The Ohio River Valley

The New York-New Jersey record, however, cannot compare with the overwhelming series of narratives issuing from one place in the United States, the Ohio River Valley.

Over twenty years ago, by digging into the back issues of the Louisville, Kentucky, *Courier-Journal*, I discovered one of those gems that has kept me pondering its meaning for two decades. The interesting little item was in the 24 October 1878 issue. A "Wild Man of the Woods" was captured, supposedly, in Tennessee, and then placed on exhibit in Louisville. The creature was described as being six feet, five inches tall, and having eyes twice the normal size. His body was "covered with fish scales." This 1878 article now makes some sense.

And then almost a hundred years later, again near Louisville, there are more stories of reptilian entities. In October 1975, near Milton, Kentucky, Clarence Cable reported a "giant lizard" was roaming the forests near his automobile junkyard. Author Peter Guttilla described the creature Cable surprised as "about fifteen feet long, had a foot-long forked tongue, and big eyes that bulged something like a frog's. It was dull-white with black-and-white stripes across its body with quarter-size speckles over it."

On-site field investigations by Mark A. Hall, however, indicated this "giant lizard" ran bipedally, according to other Trimble County, Kentucky witnesses. The Ohio River is Louisville's, Milton's, and Trimble county's northern boundary.

On 21 August 1955, near Evansville, Indiana, Mrs. Darwin Johnson was almost pulled forever into the depths of the Ohio River. In what seems to have been a very close meeting with one of these creatures,

Mrs. Johnson, of Dogtown, Indiana, was swimming with her friend Mrs. Chris Lamble about fifteen feet from shore when suddenly something grabbed her from under the surface. It felt like the "hand" had huge claws and "furry" (or scaly?) palms. It came up from behind her, grabbed her left leg, gripped her knee, and pulled her under. She kicked and fought herself free. It pulled her under again. Although both women could not see the thing, they were screaming and yelling to scare it away. Finally, Mrs. Johnson lunged for Mrs. Lamble's inner tube, and the loud "thump" apparently scared "it" away, and "it" released its grip. Back on shore, Mrs. Johnson received treatment for her scratches and marks on her leg.

Fortean investigator Terry Colvin passed on the information that Mrs. Johnson had a palm-print-shaped green stain below her knee that could not be removed, and it remained for several days. (Interestingly, Colvin learned the Johnsons were visited by an individual who identified himself as an Air Force colonel who took voluminous notes and warned them not to talk further about the incident. Of course, this sounds so similar to a "Man-In-Black" encounter that it goes almost without saying.)

For anyone who has seen *Creature from the Black Lagoon*, the Ohio River encounter of Mrs. Darwin Johnson is already familiar, for her attack was foreshadowed in that movie. John Baxter in his *Science Fiction in the Cinema*, recounts those moments:

> "A key scene of the film is when heroine (Julie Adams) enters the water for a swim, unaware that the creature is swimming just below her, admiring. Shots looking up towards the surface show the girl penetrating a Cocteau-like mirror, her white suit with its accentuated breasts, her choreographed leg movements all overtly sexual. Gliding beneath her, twisting lasciviously in a stylized representation of sexual intercourse, the creature, his movements brutally masculine and powerful, contemplates his ritual bride, though his passion does not reach its peak until the girl performs some underwater ballet movements, explicitly erotic poses that excite the Gill-Man to reach out and clutch at her murmuring legs."

The Gill-Man, the first Creature of the Black Lagoon, is presented in the film, according to Baxter, "As a force of elemental power, not maliciously evil but 'other-directed,' a fragment of a world where our ideas of morality have no relevance." We can only speculate that the same may be true of the very "real" Creatures from the Black Lagoon.

Loveland's Trolls and Frogman

From Evansville, Indiana's 1955 watery attack to Loveland, Ohio's 1955 case of the "trolls under the bridge," the story continues along the Ohio River Valley. Leonard H. Springfield's inquiry into the "affair under the bridge" is perhaps well-known to most readers.

In March 1955, after a guard had been placed at the bridge and after the F.B.I. had investigated, Ted Bloecher started talking to the businessman who had seen the four, little three-foot-tall creatures with frog's faces.

The elements of the case have been well documented in the ufological literature, but there is one point I would like to make that for years may have misled Forteans interested in such matters. The famous drawing of the "trolls under the bridge," with their lopsided chests, was sketched by Stringfield based on his *impression* of what was seen and was not drawn under the direction of the witness. The exact description of the 1955-Loveland "trolls" could more properly place them in Fortean creature chronicles than in UFO books. The frog-like nature of Loveland's 1955 beasts is reinforced by the sightings from near there for 1972. In March of that year, on two separate occasions, two Ohio policemen saw what has become known as the "Loveland Frogman." Investigated by Ron Schaffner and Richard Mackey, these researchers interviewed the officers involved but have not published their names, instead using the fictitious names "Williams" and "Johnson."

The first incident took place at 1:00 A.M. on 3 March 1972, on a clear, cold night. Officer Williams was on route to Loveland, via Riverside Road, when he thought he saw a dog beside the road. But then the "thing" stood up, its eyes illuminated by the car lights, looked at him for an instant, turned, and leapt over a guardrail. Williams saw it go down an embankment into the Little Miami River, a mere fifteen or so miles from the Ohio River. He described the thing as weighing about sixty pounds, about three to four feet tall, having a textured leathery skin, and a face like a frog or lizard. Williams went on to the police station and returned with Officer Johnson to look for evidence of the creature. They turned up scrapemarks leading down the side of the small hill near the river.

On approximately 17 March 1972, Officer Johnson was driving outside of Loveland when he had a similar experience. Seeing an animal lying in the middle of the road, he stopped to remove what he thought was a dead critter. Instead, when the officer opened his squeaky car door, the animal got up into a crouched position like a football player. The creature hobbled to the guardrail and lifted its leg over, while constantly looking at Johnson. Perhaps it was the funny smirk on its face, but Johnson decided to shoot at it. He missed, he figured, since the thing didn't slow down. Johnson later told how he felt it was more upright than the way Williams described it. One area farmer told investigators he saw a large, frog-like or lizard-like creature during the same month of the officers' sightings.

And that is the end of the stories to date.

Temporal Teleportation?

The evidence from the Ohio River Valley, therefore, is rather strong for these Creatures from the Black Lagoon being more reptile than man. Just exactly what these animals are, however, is anyone's guess, but the time teleportation theories expressed in John Michell and Robert Rickard's *Living Wonders* could give us some crazy insights into what may be happening. What if these creatures were transporting themselves back in time from some future portal?

Dale Russell, a Canadian paleontologist, has of late promoted the idea that reptiles had/have as much a possibility to evolve an intelligent, bipedal form as did the mammals. His drawings of this animal look suspiciously like the composite picture we get from the sightings of the Ohio Valley/Black Lagoon creatures. Are these beasts future time travelers lost in some time/space warp? Or are they infrequent visitors?

Or do you feel more comfortable with the idea there is a breeding population of scaly, manlike, upright creatures lingering along the edges of some of America's swamps?

Something is out there. That's for sure.

7

THE RAILS
Phantom Trains

. . . luminous things that used to be called will-o'-the-wisps. They come and they go, and their reappearances in a small region make me think of other localized repetitions that we have noted. —Charles Fort

The corn was getting high near those Kansas Pacific Railroad tracks, late that Tuesday in July. J.F. Timmons had hired some men to work near his Edwardsville area farm. Not expecting anything unusual thereabouts, Timmons had left the dozen section men to do their work. After a while, however, the wind began to blow, and the air seemed to change. All of a sudden, storm clouds appeared over the horizon, and everyone knew they had better get out of there in a hurry. Soon the men had their handcar on the railroad tracks, and they started full speed for town. They had only gone a short distance when everyone saw what they thought was a locomotive rounding a curve. Quickly, they all jumped off the car and yanked it from the tracks. What the men then saw was not what they had anticipated. In Timmons' words:

> Whatever it was came down the track giving off a volume of dense smoke with occasional flashes resembling a headlight in the center of smoke. It came three-fourths of a mile from where they first saw it, then

turned off the track at a pile of cordwood, went round it once, then went off in a southwesterly direction, through a thick wood.

What was this, a recent UFO seen near some Kansas railroad tracks? While it may be too early to specifically answer that question, let us look at the context in which I found this story. This report from 1878, within the lore of America, has been placed with others like it under the heading, "phantom trains" or "ghost trains."

(courtesy of the Institute of Fortean Studies)

The American Railroads. A long tradition of phantom train accounts tells of ghostly engines coming out of billowing clouds of smoke, looking as solid as this old locomotive, then disappearing into thin air. Often, witnesses describe how the phantom train crashes, but never a trace of a wreck is found. The phenomenon of these ghosts of the tracks is one that appears to have an underlying relationship to the tales of spook lights and haunts seen near railroads.

A Pervasive Phenomenon

In terms of spookiness, perhaps nothing can challenge the lone wailing of a distant train in the empty air of a quiet rural setting. As the listener strains to hear the next banshee-like screech of the iron monster, the eyes try to pick out the faraway beam of light from the headlamp of the expected train. But people have waited for just such a slowly approaching train, only to then *hear* a ghost engine crash or *see* passing in front of them a haunting shell of unreal railroad coaches and their skeletal passengers. Yet the observers search for but never find a trace of wreckage. Ghost or phantom trains are heard and seen from one end of America to the other, but no one can easily explain the source of the phenomena. The witnesses are especially baffled. (There is some evidence that the phenomena may be international. From Burma, reports of a phantom train heard blowing its whistle, steaming along, and then crashing from the fallen River Kwai Bridge circulated in 1958. Prisoners of war who worked on the railway said they had heard the ghost train since shortly after the British bombed the bridge, knocking a Japanese train into a ravine below.)

As Mrs. Kirk Lowry noted years after her initial 1906 North Carolina phantom train sighting: "I saw that light with my own eyes and heard the whistle. Where the ghost train came from or where it went to, I'll never know. But it went by our house almost every night 'til we moved away."

As a form of unexplained phenomena, phantom trains have been difficult to categorize, so they are usually just lumped with the hodge-podge of other strange earth-traveling vehicles supposedly from some other reality. These include the mysterious white vans seen near cattle mutilations, the black Cadillacs driven by the weird Men-in-Black (MIBs), or the funny reports of phantom covered wagons from the American West.

The phantom train reports, however, are especially interesting to me for one major reason. They stay put. Although not the most frequent category of ghostly vehicles (I'm certain the black cars filled with MIBs would win this honor), phantom trains have the distinction of being mechanical ghosts with a more or less stable location. The phantom trains, therefore, tend to be analogous to spook lights, or even the ghosts in certain haunted houses, because of their seeming loyalty to one particular spot. In *Mysterious America* some of the locations of spook lights from around the nation are listed. As stated at the head of that collection, spook lights are "mysterious, usually mobile globes of illumination seemingly attached to, and appearing periodically at specific locations." The phantom trains (see appendix I) are likewise mysterious mobile lights attached to a specific location, but they also manifest other characteristics, such as making noises. Furthermore, sometimes a more complete body of an engine or coaches are sighted, as opposed to the will-o'-the-wisp-type structures of the spook lights.

Periodic Reappearances

Like the spook lights, according to local traditions, some phantom trains appear to witnesses at recurring intervals or times. Some of these reappearances are quite elaborate. Take, for example, the frequent sightings of Lincoln's funeral train. According to an article from the 1920s, in the Albany, New York, *Evening Times*:

> Regularly in the month of April, about midnight the air on the tracks becomes very keen and cutting. On either side of the tracks it is warm and still. Every watchman, when he feels the air, slips off the track and sits down to watch. Soon the pilot engine of the Lincoln's funeral train passes with long, black streamers and with a band of black instruments playing dirges, grinning skeletons sitting all about.
>
> It passes noiselessly. If it is moonlight, clouds come over the moon as the phantom train goes by. After the pilot engine passes, the funeral train itself with flags and streamers rushes past. The track seems covered with black carpet, and the coffin is seen in the center of the car, while all about it in the air and on the train behind are vast numbers of blue-coated men, some with coffins on their backs, others leaning upon them.
>
> If a real train were passing its noise would be hushed as if the phantom train rode over it. Clocks and watches always stop as the phantom train goes by and when looked at are five to eight minutes behind.
>
> Everywhere on the road about April 27 watches and clocks are suddenly found to be behind.

The ghost of Lincoln's funeral train is a good illustration of the revisitations of such phenomena. A common factor of the reappearing phantom trains is their tragic tone. Trains and stretches of track involved in deaths, accidents, and wrecks are the ones that foster the periodically repeating ghosts. And the phantom trains may have a corner on the twenty-sevenths of April as well. I note the Ghost of the Stateville, North Carolina wreck reappears on April twenty-sevenths.

Historically, phantom train accounts have been recorded only since the advent of the railroads. Of course, I expect someday someone will find an ancient pre-railroading tale of a phantom train scaring the daylights out of some slightly upset locals. After all, the airships of the 1890s certainly appeared before such things were really flying through the skies. But for now, we must be content with the reports from the 1800s to present.

And the encounters do continue. As recently as 1941 in North Carolina, 1958 in Massachusetts, and 1974 in Connecticut, the ghosts of the tracks have been part of local witnesses' experiences. The stories may be as detailed as the North Carolina woman who heard the victims' screams of a phantom wreck or as thin as the bells and signals going off at a RR crossing, as in the recent Connecticut incident.

Connections and Explanations

So how are we to deal with these accounts, old and new, of ghostly railroad trains throughout the land? Has anyone come up with any thoughts on the matter? How would a Fortean attempt to fit these accounts into the cosmos? What related unexplainables might have some hidden insights for these stories?

In general, phantom train accounts have drifted into the archives of various folklorists, and little attention has been given to them in recent years. I believe this may be an unfortunate oversight. Perhaps it is reflective of the decline in the use of trains as a frequent form of long distance transportation. Or it may simply be the product of relabeling on the part of witnesses and recorders of the phenomena. Perhaps phantom trains are still being seen but witnesses, newspapers, and even investigators into the unknown have grouped them under a new heading.

The Vestigia Study

The growing body of articles and scholarly discussions on ghost lights and spook lights has demonstrated that phenomenon's unique attraction to streams, groves of trees, roads, certain fields, mountains, *and railroads*.

Some answers to the mystery of phantom trains may be within these recent studies of spook lights. One of the best surveys of an active spook light site, indeed, is the examination of the light seen along one mile of railroad tracks in Washington Township, Morris

(courtesy of Robert E. Jones/Vestigia)

Washington Township, New Jersey. To obtain photographs of the spook light reported along a one-mile stretch of railroad track in Morris County, the organization Vestigia had to employ the use of infrared equipment. (Photographs obtained in such a manner always appear to be foggy and out-of-focus, but in reality show a range of detail undetectable to the unaided human eye.)

Vestigia began their attempts to catch the spook light on infrared film during the fall of 1976. The light would often appear at night and bob or sway from side to side in the manner of a swinging lantern, giving rise to the ghostly tales of a departed railman haunting the tracks. When the light was approached, it vanished, sometimes reappearing at a distant spot along the rail. This photograph was taken on 22 April 1977, when the light, seen as a globe of white at the end of the tracks here, was visible to the Vestigia observers.

County, New Jersey, by the research group Vestigia. As Dr. C. Louis Wiedemann described it in that society's newsletter, at night the mystery light would "bob and sway from side to side in the manner of a swinging lantern, and when approached it vanishes, sometimes reappearing at a distant point." This New Jersey light, like the Maco Light in North Carolina, and many others, has always and only been associated with railroad tracks. While investigating the Bridgewater Triangle, I discovered that the Raynham, Massachusetts spook light appeared regularly every January over the railroad tracks behind the dog racing stadium. Numerous examples of spook light sites near or over railroad lines do exist. (Please refer to appendix I for their locations.)

(courtesy of Robert E. Jones/Vestigia)

One of the most bizarre spook light infrared photographs obtained by Vestigia is this one taken on 27 September 1977. The light was caught by accident while the researchers were obtaining a trial shot of two Vestigia members walking the tracks. The light was not *visible to the eye. The mystery light, however, clearly can be seen behind the two people in this infrared photograph.*

Vestigia feels strongly that the metallic railroad tracks are an important factor in these accounts. From their experiments and photographic evidence, they have put forth a novel theory. Vestigia sees spook lights as the products of electricity produced by the squeezing of certain minerals during earthquakes and minor earth movements. These so-called piezoelectric effects would result in spook lights and be directly caused by the stress of geological fault, piezoelectric-conducting minerals (such as quartz), and the accumulation of the resulting electrical buildup and discharge through the metal tracks oriented along the fault. While the relationship between earthquake lights, recently determined to be caused by seismic activity, and spook lights is one of cloudy conjecture, the research conducted by Vestigia is worthy of study. But questions do remain.

Electromagnetic Sounds

Interestingly, a new theory for the reason that fireballs, those infrequent giant meteors, make noises as they pass overhead may have something to do with the phantom train phenomena. Fireball sounds are not supposed to be heard at the same time they are seen, good physics would have us believe, because, of course, light travels faster than sound. This is not the case, however.

As Pam Weintraub points out in the April 1985 issue of *Omni*, the hiss of the fireball has called upon physicists to come up with some novel solutions. Colin Keay of the University of New Castle, Australia feels he has found the answer. In a nutshell, he thinks the fireball going through the air on its descent to earth is pushing hot gases, a plasma, in front of it trapping the earth's magnetic field. As the meteor slows down, its plasma is dissipated, and the magnetic force field is released in the form of extremely low-frequency electromagnetic radiation. This radiation, of course, travels at the speed of light and reaches the fireball observer at the same time the person sees the meteor. The force field causes objects to vibrate near the individual, and thus they hear the whoosh, hiss, or roar of the monster meteor. Another researcher, Allen Frey, even thinks the electromagnetic energy may be vibrating the liquid in the internal ear.

For us, the whole idea that plasma may be able to interact, store, and actually create waves of electromagnetic surges could explain various segments of the phantom train reports. And we especially note Keay has said that people with loose clothing, steel rimmed glasses, and frizzy hair are creating environments in which more vibrations exist and more noises are heard. Are not the clothing, glasses, and hair styles more suggestive of the good ole' days than most modern dress?

The plasma explanations of Vestigia and the electromagnetic force field thoughts of Colin Keay perhaps should be combined in future examinations of spook light and phantom train incidents.

Haunted Attachments

But what of spook lights that seem to indicate more of a haunted attachment to an old railroad bed than to the actual metal rails? Exactly such a circumstance was revealed in March 1951 at Suffolk in Nansemond County, Virginia. After several people saw what was labeled "The Light," investigating Deputy Sheriff Hurley Jones also saw it. He described The Light as resembling a single automobile headlamp heading right towards you. Jeston Reid, sixty-two years old, who lives on Jackson Road, told investigators at the time that his father told him he saw the spook light some seventy-five years ago. Raleigh Outland stated he had seen it all his life. He noted that sometimes it stays "right in the middle of the road, about five feet off the ground," and at other times veers off to the side of Jackson Road. The head of the state troopers locally, Sergeant W.S. Dameron said: "It's a bright light that looks exactly like a *train coming down a track*." (emphasis added!)

Over three hundred cars showed up in March of 1951 to look for an answer to the mystery of The Light. More serious investigations into the matter brought forth the discovery that the old Jackson and Whaleyville Railroad ran down the strip that has since been renamed the Jackson Road. Deputy Sheriff Beale, seventy-five, recalled that a railroad flagman was killed on the line, in about 1912, and many folks believed it was the flagman with his lantern that was haunting the old railroad bed. But general agreement in Suffolk County is that the light had been seen long before that occurred.

In our research into old railroad grades, we have discovered there is an exact science to their construction. The bottom layer is the subgrade, which is usually earth, rock, or clay, and is about two or three feet deep, except in bogs when its depth may be twenty feet. This is covered with the subballast layer of porous material, like sand or cinders, to about one foot in depth. For our discussion, the next layer, the ballast, seems to be the most important. This plateau is made up of small, crushed stones; cinders from coal-fired locomotives; and interestingly, in the vicinity of steel mills, broken slag from the smelter. What is the importance of this metallic layer in the reports of spook lights seen over old railroad grades? Or what is the legacy of the drop from a high of 254,000 rail miles in 1916 to today's total of about 160,000—and those unused grades' long history of wrecks and accidents? Are the old beds haunted? Or are they electromagnetic conductors?

Spook lights or phantom trains? Or ghosts? The fine lines between the various pigeonholes we try to create for the phenomena are destroyed by the data. Our feeble speculations are made uncomfortable by the accounts. One cozy file is created and along comes another piece of the puzzle, another new story that just won't fit easily. But the human condition demands answers and nice filing systems, so the search goes on to suggest insights that push the parameters of our understanding.

Phantom Lantern Carriers and More

Theories of a paranormal or psychic basis have, therefore, also merited consideration over the years. So very many spook lights have occurred along or near railroad tracks that the common folkloric explanation is that the light is the swinging lantern of a dead trainman. Dr. Weidemann noted this is the explanation given for the origin of the New Jersey mystery light. As I have toured the country, I too have heard this explanation from railroad spook light sites in the East to ghostly haunted railroad trestles in the West. Some psychic investigators have sensed and thus explained spook lights in terms of deceased spirits. Apparently, we are told, phenomena labeled phantom trains could also be viewed as the ghosts who have passed before. Paranormal thoughts on these subjects, along with the reports of mysterious globes of light in cemeteries and in old haunted houses, constitute a growing body of the psychic literature. Hilary Evans' excellent examination of the overlapping connections between such phenomena, stated nicely in the title of his book, *Visions * Apparitions * Alien Visitors: A Comparative Study of the Entity Enigma* (Aquarian, London, 1984), demonstrates the growing awareness of the underlying oneness of such reports. Might it also be that nonanimate projections such as phantom trains are only one of innumerable examples in a similar nonentity vein?

Railroad UFOs

As students of ufology will note, some phantom trains remind one of flying saucers of the rails. They flash various colored lights, often dart about with great speed, and as we saw from the Lincoln train incident, sometimes have electromagnetic effects and time warping phenomena associated with them. UFO sightings, fairylore, and some psychic case histories have long held evidence of time displacements and the disruption of energy forcefields. Not too surprisingly, then, here we find the same kinds of events occurring during the visitations of phantom trains.

Can anything be gained from throwing the phantom train reports in with the UFO accounts? They even share many of the more bizarre characteristics of UFOs, such as the encounters with some strange "occupants." One of the most bizarre phantom train occupant cases happened during one of last century's Marshall Pass, Colorado sightings. The report in question mentions that a "tall man" was seen gesturing wildly atop one of the coaches. Meanwhile, the railman witness noticed the ghost train's engineer was madly laughing and had a face "like dough." These "individuals" are not exactly the kinds of "people" one would want to meet in a narrow, lonely Rocky Mountain pass. Can you imagine experiencing something that probably would find its way into today's papers as: "THE PILLSBURY DOUGHBOY GOES WEST, THANKS TO PHANTOM TRAIN"?

The Merging Phenomena

Phantom trains do have elements of several types of phenomena. So what gives? What is this—fairyland revisited? The netherworld of UFOs and Rip Van Winkle? It is almost as if the phantom trains, with their unique facets of giant rolling locomotives and shrill whistles, have carved out a niche in the folklore literature but would fit comfortably in Fortean studies. As we have begun to discover, the oneness between such accounts often outweighs the seeming differences. The phantom trains fade nicely into spook light, UFO, and haunted location sightings. The differences may rest more within the witnesses' interpretations, frames of reference, and historical context. Examinations of the phenomenon of phantom trains and its common denominators with other unexplainables certainly has indicated to me a relationship beyond what has been acknowledged thus far.

That the huge, smoking phantom locomotives, ghosts on the tracks, are still steaming their way down the rails of America seems to emerge from the data. What they are called today, what they "really" are, where they come from, how they got here, and how they are related to similar phenomena are all questions whose answers, for now, must remain in some ghostly tunnel in a faraway mountain. Still, the chance remains for you to see one of these old steam phantoms on the rails near your home; consult the list in appendix I, and let me know if you have any luck.

8

THE HILLS
Strange Stone Forts

When we come upon assurances that a mystery has been solved, we go on investigating. —Charles Fort

Mysteries surrounding the origins and meanings of grand stone monuments, such as Easter Island's great statues, Stonehenge, Malta's megalithic structures, or even the Pyramids, have fired the imaginations of generations of thinkers. These bizarre relics in exotic locations naturally lend themselves to thoughts of ancients of greater wisdom and other arcane notions. But few North Americans have known about or considered the mysteries of the "stone forts" near their own towns. Extensively and routinely continuous walls of stone, some looking like fortifications and thus called "forts" by the locals, are found from California to Massachusetts. My interest in the subject goes back many years.

One of the first articles I wrote, in the 1960s, was on the stone forts of Illinois. After bibliographic searches, hours examining area maps, and rigorous field work, I had discovered that the walls at the tip of that state were mysteriously aligned. Since then, I have viewed similar structures in Georgia and California and deeply researched others across the nation. Let's journey to some of these strange forts of America.

Southern Illinois' Forts

I fell in love with southern Illinois when I first traveled there. It is one of those places of smoothly rolling hills and calm vistas. I remember vividly the first time I went looking for the stone forts of the area, topping the crest of a small upheaval in the land and being greeted with a burst of yellow from a vast field of daffodils. The beauty of this land, which has more in common with areas south of the Mason-Dixon line than its Yankee history might indicate, would be enough to fill anyone with wonder. But the mysteries of the region make it a doubly enchanting place to explore. And many before me had viewed the anomaly, that is, the stone forts. Since the late eighteenth century, the stone forts of southern Illinois have been a mystery to the immigrant Europeans and Africans. Colonel Leonard White noted the walls when he toured the region shortly after the Revolutionary War. Down through the years, discussions of the forts such as in Moyer's 1934 article, "The Seven Wonders of Egypt," have continued in obscure historical society journals. (This section of Illinois has the unique feature of being called "Egypt" or "Little Egypt," adding another level of intrigue to the story.) Over and over again the wondrous nature of the structures was discussed because, simply, no one knew what to make of them.

At least ten pre-Columbian stone forts are known to exist in the hills of southern Illinois. There may be others, the walls of which have been razed down to ground level; one of the more recent finds was made when the foundation courses were accidently observed. These chance finds have many people wondering if the known walls are just the tip of the iceberg. Some researchers from Southern Illinois University think there is a strong probability that several smaller walls may exist in the remote backwash of the Shawnee National Forest, an area of concentrated weirdness from sightings of Bigfoot-type creatures and phantom panthers to the usual run of UFO stories. Of the ten mystery walls located thus far, it is interesting to note that a large number of them seem to be found near the Devil's Kitchen area (refer to *Mysterious America* for a discussion of the implications of "devil's names" and bizarre locations).

A Mysterious Alignment

These walled structures, forming a rough alignment between the Mississippi and Ohio rivers, have one striking feature in common—

each is located on top of a high bluff where it projects outward. From the rear, they can be approached easily over gently sloping ground. On every other side, the structures border on sheer cliffs. This would suggest that their primary purpose was as forts; however, only one (that near Stonefort in Saline County) has a water supply within it. Stone cairns and stone-lined pits are found beside the entrance gateways of all.

They are constructed of dry-stone masonry, using loose stones of moderate size. Early records, and the recollections of very old people still living, indicate that the walls were originally six feet high and about as wide. They are now greatly diminished, as a result of farmers hauling the stones away. Some, such as Stonefort previously mentioned, were over six hundred feet in length. The Stonefort wall also forms half of an accurate ellipse with axes of 450 and 190 feet. It is difficult to understand how this structure could have been so accurately laid out if the area were as heavily forested at the time as it is now. The amount of labor necessary to build such walls is staggering.

Scholarly Conjectures and Other Fantasies

What were these forts used for? Who built them? How old are they? Well, the answers are totally unknown. But, of course, that has not stopped many from speculating. From other parts of the country various stories exist as to the shadowy "ancient ones" who came "before" and constructed the forts. Such conjectures exist at one end of a continuum. Meanwhile, there are more traditional theories just as unsatisfying.

For example, archaeologists at the University Museum, Southern Illinois University, believe that some form of prehistoric Indians built the walls. Because some of the artifacts found at one site, Hog Bluff, seem to match fragments found at the Kincaid Mound's so-called "Lewis Focus," the wall builders are labeled the "Lewis People." The Lewis People are envisioned as a kind of underdeveloped Native American tribal group existing in Illinois before the advent of the Mississippians who "possessed a better way of exploiting the environment," according to archaeologists Brieschke and Rackerby's 1973 *Outdoor Illinois* article. The pair go on to note:

> The crux of the theory says that it was the contact of these two differing groups during late Woodland times that brought on a situation of

> competition for the same resources. This competition took the form of open hostilities with the Mississippians pushing the "Lewis People" back up into the hills with their final conquest and/or gradual absorption into the Mississippian social framework. The "stone forts" then were part of the defensive system used by the "Lewis People." These sites were a place where they could seek refuge when in danger from attack. At other times they occupied rock shelters and open sites in this upland region.

As can be seen by the use of quotations around the phrase Lewis People, this bit of anthropological theorizing is nothing more than using one mystery to explain another. Sort of like saying all cattle mutilations are caused by beings from flying saucers, except the authorities in this case have the backing of a university. Frankly, I think it is time to be a bit more careful about accepting such academically recommended answers. Myth-making appears to issue from the halls of ivy just as surely as it does from the filing cabinets of collectors of curiosities.

And there is plenty of room for theorizing about the walls. Similar stone walls or forts exist elsewhere in the eastern United States in Alabama, Connecticut, Georgia, Indiana, Kentucky, Missouri, New York, Ohio, Tennessee, and West Virginia. The walls are not to be confused with the prehistoric geometrical structures of stone and earth, the so-called earthworks and mounds, found throughout the East, supposedly constructed by the elusive Mound-Builders. The walls are very different, unique, and probably even more ancient. While their wonder does captivate a few Fortean researchers in some locations, most local residents usually do not even know they have a real life mystery at their doorstep. An exception is Georgia's strange stone fort.

On to Georgia

Thousands of people annually climb the easy path to the 2,832 foot apex of Fort Mountain, Georgia. The wall at the top runs a total length of 885 feet from east to west. It ranges in height from two to seven feet, but as I observed when I examined the site, the height was undoubtedly much higher as the whole of the wall is surrounded by

(photograph by Libbet Cone)

Fort Mountain, Georgia. The mystery walls of this site overlook some of the most beautiful country in the South. Was this strange stone fort built by moon-eyed, short, blond people, as some of the Cherokee oral traditions state?

fallen rocks. Like the walls of Illinois, near the Georgia wall are pits, twenty nine in all, but unlike the midwestern versions, these ancient "foxholes" are large enough for a half dozen fair-sized men to hide in.

When I visited Fort Mountain, with Georgia associate A. Jeanette Sarbo, the day was clear and the view unforgettable. Just as Robert Shackleton had written in 1893: "Other mountains stretch off into the distance, while below are tree-covered slopes and rocky precipices, and mile after mile of forests and fields and farms. The eye never wearies of the glorious sight, and as one glances over the magnificent expanse he tries to imagine what were the thoughts of the mysterious people who centuries since dwelt on this height."

Who Built the Fort?

Indeed, fantasies about who built Fort Mountain have been interesting and involved. The thoughts on the matter have ranged from the notion that the Cherokees fashioned it to serve as a honeymoon haven to the idea that this same local tribal group built it to keep the Creeks out. As with the Illinois walls, no springs or other sources of water are found within the area. Any type of romantic or military strategist among the Cherokee would have certainly taken survival into account. Also, there has never been one shred of evidence, be it artifact or skeletal, that any Native Americans, prehistoric or otherwise ever used this so-called fortification site. In the realm of legends, two vie for our attention in the lore of Fort Mountain. The first is the tale of Prince Madoc.

Prince Madoc is an enigmatic figure, sort of a Welsh Ulysses. Although overlooked by most historians, Madoc sailed from Wales with two hundred men in eleven ships and landed at what is now Mobile Bay, Alabama in A.D. 1170—beating Columbus by 322 years. The Daughters of the American Revolution even have a commemoration marker located in Mobile Bay noting the event. The best book on the subject is *Madoc and the Discovery of America* by Richard Deacon, perhaps the foremost espionage scholar alive today. The document is an exciting mixture of "Welsh Indians" discovered by later Europeans; the famed American painter George Catlin's pursuit of the "white" Indians, the Mandans; and spying among the Spaniards. In Prince Madoc's exploration of the New World, so the story goes, he built forts from Georgia to Tennessee, and Fort Mountain was one of these. But the evidence for such a claim appears to be based mostly on negative stances and ethnocentric assumptions. The argument seems to follow the logic that since these forts are built with "patience and labour" so that "too much cannot be said in praise of both the genius and the skill of the men who constructed the fortifications," they had to be fashioned "not . . . by Indians, but by a past people greatly skilled in arts," which for Deacon means "Europeans."

But perhaps the other major legend associated with Fort Mountain has as much to say about the "past people" as this speculation on Prince Madoc and his Welshmen. An old Cherokee legend credits a race of moon-eyed, blond, small, light-skinned people who worshipped the sun as the wall builders. The site, in this theory, therefore, is primarily seen as a ritual structure having more in common with Stonehenge. To date, no one has applied astroarchaeological research to any of the forts in America, and something may come of some investigations in this direction. For now, we will leave Fort Mountain with the note that it does run from east to west, just as one might expect a wall built by worshippers of the rising and setting sun.

California's Mystery Walls

Whereas the walls and forts of the East are frequently written off as colonial in origin, or in some obtuse way, as being built by the Mound Builders (as if, once again, explaining one highly documented unknown with another less academically accepted one will make the mystery disappear). Way out West these explanations just do not hold water. The very history and nature of northern California defeat these easy and understandably acceptable (to some) East Coast explanations. But the shocking fact is, the walls are mirror images of their eastern counterparts.

During November 1984, thanks to my California colleagues Judy Levy and Nora Contini, to the kind efforts of Tilden Park Ranger Tim Gordon, and to local wall sleuth Russell Swanson, I examined the Mystery Walls of Berkeley and Oakland and was given invaluable data on similar walls found at nearby Mission Peak.

These largely ignored walls of the East Bay area near San Francisco are made of huge, basalt boulders weighing one ton or more. Most of the examinations of the walls have centered on those in Tilden Regional Park. Because of the ease of access, most researchers look at those on Vollmer Peak (which was formerly called Old Baldy before a political decision was made to name the peak after a police chief). Even easier to find are two large boulders in Tilden's Botanical Garden. These two stones were formerly part of the wall south of the Garden that was mindlessly destroyed by short-sighted construction during the 1930s. (Interestingly, in 1969 a buried water tunnel, of unknown origin, was found near the Botanical Garden, according to the appropriately named John Waters, who was there the day the tunnel was uncovered. Anomalous tunnels and hidden water courses have often been associated with other megalithic sites, such as Stonehenge, around the globe.)

Finding the wall on Vollmer is not an easy feat, but as Russell Swanson drove his ancient, white Skylark nearer the peak, I knew I had chosen the right guide. Russ was tired; tired of the anthropologists who won't come up to the mountain to see the wall; tired of reading in tabloids about how ancient astronauts had built the walls; tired of hearing folks say the Ohlone Indians had built the walls when he knew the well-fed, peaceful, laid-back tribe had no desire to construct over twenty miles of walls that started and ended nowhere. White-haired, crusty, and kind, Russell Swanson, a fifty-five-year-old trade show organizer, had had his fill of the theories about Toltecs, Atlanteans, lost tribes, Spanish missionaries, and visitors from outer space. Russ was willing to imagine a pre-Columbian contact from China or Japan, but deep down he was not going to commit himself to anything other than the fact the walls were there—they are a mystery, and no one knows who built them. As his dearly beloved car drew closer to Vollmer, I knew this man could ponder the enigma of the walls in a way close to my own approach to mysteries, and I was happy my brief Fortean tour of the Bay area had found time for Russell Swanson.

Once Russ, my wife Libbet, and I had arrived at the wall, I could see how casual park strollers had missed this site. Hidden by poison oak, on the crest of a small slope, the wall was on the other side of a barbed wire fence, and really on water district land, not park land. Naturally this worries Russ. What is the future of these walls? Barely treated as curiosities by the park officials, the water district people do not even understand their value. In the past, Russ noted, road crews and vandals have destroyed vast sections of the Vollmer and nearby walls, using them in construction because of their availability or rolling them down hills to get them out of the "way" or for purely mischievous reasons.

The walls look so similar to those I had viewed in Illinois and Georgia as to be identical. And here too were the pits I had seen at the sites of those states' walls. In Georgia, the pits had been so big that Libbet and a friend could easily crouch in them, but these in California were much smaller, although exactly alike in configuration. This revelation was news to Russell, as no one else had made this connection.

Sinister Rumblings

As we walked all over the side of Vollmer Peak, during the next two hours, Russ told me about the other nearby sites. Another section of the wall is found in Sibley Regional Park, near Round Top Peak. Vollmer and Round Top are two of the East Bay's highest hills. Farther south, near Fremont's Mission Peak, one of the longest existing sections of the wall stretches across several miles of sloping countryside.

While Russell may have sounded a bit alarmed about the future of the walls in the Berkeley and Oakland area, these walls near Fremont and Milpitas have him deeply worried. Apparently all out war has been declared between local residents and all interlopers, including the good and bad folks interested in the walls. Locals' cows get shot regularly and so do hikers. Parking and hiking in the Mission Peak Regional Reserve is prohibited, but that does not stop individuals from invading park or private property. Someone even tried to crate off part of the wall. The Regional Reserve officials are so worried by the DMZ-type conditions, they routinely send helicopters over the area. In the last few years, several people have been murdered up on the flank of Mission Peak.

There is a dark and gloomy shadow around Mission Peak, California similar in many ways to the negative energy around Mount Misery, New York, which John Keel spoke of in his *The Mothman Prophecies*. The past days of Mission Peak have been no different than the recent ones. Russell Swanson observed that the largest massacre of Indians in California history occurred at the mission that gave Mission Peak its name.

Pondering a Key Discovery

Mission Peak's wall, if saved from the struggles between its natives and visitors, may hold a key to the mystery of all the strange forts and weird walls throughout the country. It appears Russell Swanson and his associates have made a startling find. At the edge of one section of the Mission Peak wall, a circle of stones has been discovered with what looks like a solstice stone at a proper equinox point. On the side of one of the stones, etchings have revealed what looks like Ursa Major, the Big Dipper.

After ending my tour of these California walls, I was left to ponder much on my journey back to San Francisco on the ultra-modern Bay Area Rapid Transit system. Were these bygone megalithic builders identical to the builders of the walls of the East, or to even those of Western Europe? How is one to fathom the meaning of these structures in the context of this technological age? Right now it seems too early to tell what the messages of the walls are, but certainly the neglect they have experienced between the time they were built and now is ending as they become one of America's most enduring mysteries.

9

COAST TO COAST
Spooky Sites, Mystery Spots, and Magnetic Hills

I am tired of the sensible explanations that are holding back new delusions....

...Oh, yes, I have heard of 'the fourth dimension,' but I am going to do myself some credit by not lugging in that particular way of showing that I don't know what I'm writing about. —Charles Fort

I give quite a few lectures here and there about strange phenomena, and the second question people usually ask me (after the one about what I have *personally* experienced) is not a casual one to answer. Everyone wants to know where they can go see a real "spooky site," as I call them. Now, it is not a simple matter of telling folks to go to a local telephone book or a regular travel guidebook to find their neighborhood's haunted house, enchanted cemetery, or mystery location.

Spooky Sites

The spooky sites, real places with a history of poltergeists, hauntings, or other ghostly activities do exist. Indeed, I live in a house that is allegedly haunted by a woman-in-white, although I have never seen her. But others have written extensively on these places, and I shall refer you to my *Mysterious America's* regional bibliography for some good sources instead of going on and on here about such well-worn matters. Hans Holzer, a sincere and dedicated researcher, has done much to promote some well-known haunted houses, and I recommend his books. And there are other books that tackle these ghostly houses; Richard Winer's are good examples.

But there are gaps to be filled. For me, I have found some locations are more spooky than any house could ever be. As I have traveled

(courtesy of the Virginia State Travel Service)

Charles City, Virginia. One of Virginia's haunted houses is the Shirley Plantation built in 1723. The mansion has been in the Hill-Carter family for over nine generations. Stories of the eerie knockings began when a portrait of Aunt Pratt was removed from its usual location. Family members have been trying to get peace ever since. Twenty-five miles from Richmond, Shirley is a working plantation today as it always has been.

about, I have tried to keep a list of these by state/province, city/geographical indicator, and the exact "spooky site," if it has a name. I have found that, for example, the mansions of Virginia, the cemeteries of Illinois, the canyons of California have more than their fair share of hauntings. In a related vein, I have picked places for inclusion in my list like Watkins Glen, New York and Mt. Glastenbury, Vermont; they are so spooky that scores of people have vanished while merely visiting them. Other sites around the nation seem to be regular meeting grounds for ghostly entities.

I have tried to capture some of these places for you in the list in appendix II. This easy reference should quickly answer your questions about what strange places exist near where you live or visit. I identify some of the better known and least known of these locations, houses, and places in this massive list that I hope will serve you well. If you discover others, write me at P.O. Box 109, Rangeley, Maine 04970, and I'll update the list in future editions.

But before you examine the spooky sites list in appendix II, I want to spend some moments with you examining this notion of mystery spots and magnetic hills, which often *are* found in tourist guide books. Such locations are not spooky sites; to me, they are silly sidetrips. I have also included a list of these places, for easy comparison and contrast with the collection of more clearcut haunted locations. Magnetic hills and mystery spots are found in quite a few states and provinces, and I trust I have captured some of the famous ones on the list. If there are more I missed, again, let me know.

Mystery Spots

Then, without further remarks, let's take a quick trip to some of these so-called "mystery spots." The most discussed is the so-called Oregon Vortex located near Gold Hill, Oregon. Found at 4303 Sardine Creek Road, Jackson County, it is operated under the trade name "The House of Mystery" by Ernie and Irene Cooper. This vortex has been described by its proponents as being a sort of electromagnetic sphere or whirlpool 165 feet in diameter at ground level and, reportedly, extending to some 45,000 feet in the sky. Birds supposedly do not fly overhead or nest in the vortex.

For under five dollars for adults, and a discount for kids, you can go see the Oregon Vortex and House of Mystery and join the fifty-minute tour of the site. The walk is part picture-taking fun, part science, and part fantasy. The tour guide will tell you how within the vortex people lean slightly and perceptibly toward magnetic north. Everything that faces the south, the commentary continues, looks shorter. A plumb bob hangs at an acute angle. Tree limbs curve and hang in eerie ways.

The stories that go along with the tour are just as entertaining as the mini-lessons in physics. The House of Mystery is said to be the old assay office of the Great Eagle Mining Company. When a mud slide sent the office and toolshed downhill in 1907, the building landed in the midst of the Oregon Vortex. In 1914, an eccentric Scottish engineer, John Lister, bought the property. In 1930, he opened it as a tourist attraction and lived there for twenty-four years until his death. Lister allegedly conducted fourteen thousand experiments on the vortex and exchanged letters with Albert Einstein on the site. The content of the letters and results of the experiments are unknown. The tour guide tells us: "Lister burned all his records before he died because he didn't think the world was ready for what was here."

The Coopers bought the place in 1959 and have continued Lister's traditions. During the tour one can see a golf ball "roll uphill." A broom is balanced in a position on the sloping floor of the House of Mystery so that you would swear it is leaning towards the North Pole by some strange force. The Coopers note that some people even say the Vortex eases their arthritis. Irene Cooper says the place used to give her a headache, but now it gives her an income.

In the May 1981 issue of *Omni* Ray Hyman, professor of psychology, and Jerry Andrus tackled the Oregon Vortex and came away convinced everything was not what it seemed. The Vortex and the other mystery spots like it around the country, they feel, are based on optical illusions and simple but harmless magic tricks (like the balancing broom stunt). These scholars note that without proper planes of reference the human brain is tricked, and these mystery spots are filled with horizons that aren't level, corners that aren't squared, and walls that aren't vertical.

Andrus is quoted as noting that the Oregon Vortex is a "very convincing optical illusion, but that's all it is." He feels it should more properly be called a "fun house, like at the carnival." What really upsets him is that the Vortex is advertised as "an incredible scientific phenomenon" that's unexplained. Disturbed by claims of "light being warped" and such, Andrus frankly says: "That's nonsense."

The Oregon Vortex is very similar to the many mystery spots found throughout the country, and indeed, it does seem to be the granddaddy of them all. It is not taking its competition lying down, however. In the official brochure of the House of Mystery, we find these words: "It will be readily understood that, following the widespread interest in the Oregon Vortex, various attempts would be made to imitate it. The first imitation of the House of Mystery was built at Santa Cruz, California in 1941. It is unfortunate that fictitious histories, backgrounds, and explanations should be given at these imitations, but the visitor to the Oregon Vortex will immediately perceive its authenticity. It is firmly established as the World-Famous Oregon Vortex. Souvenir, novelty, and cold drink shop open during season."

When I toured the Mystery Spot at 1953 Branciforte Drive in Santa Cruz, late in 1984, I was struck by how identical it is to the Oregon Vortex. The old mining shack is there, slammed up against a hillside supposedly by a landslide. The trick with the weights, plumb bobs, and balls rolling "uphill" are all faithfully performed. Tourists snap pictures, are awed by the optical illusions, and leave another American mystery spot happy and perplexed. As the flyer for Santa Cruz's Mystery Spot says: "It's unusual, it's amazing, it's wholesome, interesting entertainment."

The mystery spots are, at least, all of these things, but are they more? Electromagnetic hotspots? Gravity anomalies? Vortices of unknown forces? The evidence, thus far, is rather thin for the extraordinary claims made by these places. And this is most clearly shown in their kin, the magnetic hills.

Magnetic Hills

The so-called magnetic, mystery, or spook hills that dot the North American countryside are also points of illusion and magic. These hills are not true unexplainables, however, just merely entertaining attractions. Some are developed to the level of tourist sideshows, most are not. These strange hills, which are supposed to defy gravity, are interesting places to take the kids, but don't go there expecting to see Fortean phenomena.

Moncton, New Brunswick's Magnetic Hill, is perhaps the most famous of the lot. It is like a magnet too, for its magnetism draws hundreds of people each year to ponder what they see and what they thought they saw. Magnetic Hill in New Brunswick makes cars, balls, skateboards, and anything round or with brakeless wheels, roll "uphill." Travelers drive out to the crest of the hill, look ahead, and see the road dip about twenty feet in the next four hundred feet, then climb again. You drive your automobile to the "bottom" of the dip, turn off the engine, don't put on the brakes, and shift the gear into neutral. Before you know it, your car will start rolling "up" the little "hill" you just came down, and at a speed of fifteen miles an hour.

The story goes that it all started back in the 1930s with a milkcart. A business-seeking milkman had stopped his horse-drawn cart at the bottom of the hill and crossed a field to see if he could make a sale. To his surprise, he turned around and found his horse, old Ned, and the milkcart halfway up the hill. The tale got around, and people have been flocking to the hill ever since.

Residents sometimes forget they have one of these magnetic hills around, and then someone is changing a flat tire, their car rolls off the jack, and straight "up" the hill. In the early forties, something like that happened at the now-and-then forgotten Spook Hill of Leominster, Massachusetts, and over one thousand cars showed up to try it out. Needless to say, a traffic jam occurred.

As you will discover if you go to one of the magnetic hills listed in appendix III, you probably will be like the 90 percent of the past drivers who visited them. They didn't care what was causing their cars to roll "uphill," they just got a kick out of it and brought their friends back the next time they came. (Are magnetic hills international? We note the Agence France-Presse carried a dispatch on 18 May 1976 from the tiny village of Djabal Moukaber, Israel. Cars, water, and footballs were rolling uphill on the nearby road to Jerusalem.) So, in the near future when you open one of those brochures like, for example, the current North Carolina Travel and Tourism Division's booklet, and read:

> MYSTERY HILL—Between Boone and Blowing Rock. This amazing natural phenomenon at Mystery House itself seems to defy the law of gravity. Objects act the opposite than normally expected. Authentic mountainlife exhibits are on the property.

Then, relax and enjoy it for what it is, a pleasant tourist attraction.

Tourists and Forteans Beware

Refer to the list of spooky sites in appendix II, however, when you want to take in one of the special places with a bit more proven and reoccurring Fortean history. Unearthly poltergeists, friendly ghosts, or even the abstract aura of strangeness are not usually haunting the "mystery spots;" the fumes of the tour buses have scared them away.

(courtesy of the Tennessee Tourist Development)

Adams, Tennessee. The presence of Tennessee's famous Bell Witch is still occasionally reported in the Bell Witch Cave on the farm that once belonged to John Bell. One of the most documented supernatural episodes in American history, the Bell Witch allegedly murdered John Bell in 1820 and harassed his daughter for much of her life. Tales of the strange happenings at the Bell farm brought Andrew Jackson himself to investigate. After a night of terror, Jackson commented, "By the eternal, I saw nothing, but I heard enough to convince me that I would rather fight the British than to deal with this torment they call the Bell Witch."

10

GAIA
Patterns

My own acceptance is that ours is an organic existence, and that our thoughts are the phenomena of its eras, quite as its rocks and trees and forms of life are; and that I think as I think, mostly, though not absolutely, because of the era I am living in.
—Charles Fort

As I write these words early in 1985, a videotape of a lecture by Peter Russell entitled *The Global Brain* is being shown on living room VCRs and on local public broadcasting stations throughout various communities of North America. Interestingly, the theme of the program is the possible effects of everyone communicating almost telepathically and empathically with each other, worldwide. In its own way, the non-changing message of the tape, played over and over again, assists the spread of its underlying epistle.

Perhaps, not coincidentally, the video has many moments that feel familiar to quite a few folks watching it. These viewers have experienced notions similar to those expressed by Russell, and whether they are readers of Shirley McLaine's latest book or Brad Steiger's *Star People*, the same messages are, of late, hitting home through different media.

The Global Organism

One insight of Russell's, which especially makes a lot of sense to Forteans, is the whole (no pun intended) section of *The Global Brain* devoted to the examination of the Earth as an organism. Now, of course, others have said the same thing recently in their own special ways—people like Jim Brandon, Bob Rickard, and Paul Winter. Discussions of *Gaia*, the ancient Greek name for the Earth goddess, are rampant today. As Brandon and Rickard have pointed out, novelist William Golding is pushing to have Gaia replace the term Earth for our planet. Golding writes: "Those who think of the world as a lifeless lump would do well to watch out. Only the other day something irritated her and with a *moue*, it may be, she wrecked cities from China to the Philippines and blew out the side of a mountain in Ecuador."

The simple and strikingly visual metaphor used by Russell, however, is as appealing and innovative as, for example, Winter's music is clear to the ear and Golding's humor is to the brain's pleasure center. Peter Russell uses the image of a flea on an elephant. Sitting there on this tough surface, the flea is aware, understands, and knows the "hairy bits, sweaty bits, and fatty bits," as Russell puts it, of his own flea-oriented world. But is this flea's neighborhood all there is? The flea leaps into the air and presently sees a new universe of ridges, hairy fields, and folds. Jumping still higher, and further away from his "home," the flea then sees it has been living on the body of a giant living thing itself, an elephant in this case.

Frankly, when I was about twelve, I remember thinking about similar notions—about the town I lived in, about this country, and about Earth. Maybe, just maybe, I thought, if we could get some distance from this existence we could see what was going on. And

Devil's Tower, Wyoming. The location of ancient tales of a giant phantom bear and the site of the movie Close Encounters of the Third Kind, *Devil's Tower has a name hinting at a history of strangeness. "Devil names" is just one of the passions pursued by Forteans, investigators of the unexplained, in seeking the patterns among the phenomena examined. Inquiry into flaps, cycles, and other games of time is another.*

(courtesy of the Wyoming Travel Commission)

what we might find is that we are only part of a large living thing. Now plenty of folks have said the Apollo pictures of this Earth from the moon have done just that. Certainly it is a step in the right direction, but there are other ways of looking at the Earth.

The Name Game Revisited

For Forteans, an enjoyable way to do this is by way of toying with cycles and patterns. In chapter 21 of *Mysterious America*, I spent some time with this passion by way of examining the "name game." I examined the discoveries and associations that several specific names (e.g., Decatur, Lafayette, Logan, McDaniel, Wetzel, Reeves) seem to be literally entwined with reoccurring mysterious incidents. It is almost as if Gaia's paranormal zones, her pimples, if you will, are someway being labeled and revisited by the phenomena, again and again. These games of the name continue; for example, Fayette County, Ohio was hit with a strange series of sheep killings in November 1984.

Other subtler examples still come to my attention. The areas named Hockomock—a peninsula and bay in Maine, a swamp and cemetery in Massachusetts, and other sites throughout New England—all have been associated with UFOs, strange lights, bizarre creatures, ghosts, disappearances, and the like. Hockomock, as well as its related forms, is an Algonquian word for "evil spirit" or "devil." Other similar Native American words have been used to label the "bedeviled places" and hint at a long-term knowledge of the spookiness of these spots. Skeptics of my arguments regarding "devil" -named places point to Anglo-Americans' expectations of something bizarre happening at a "Devil's Den," or "Devil's Kitchen." But what are we to make of the phenomenon that most local Hockomock residents, who do not understand the name has evil connotations, continue to experience concentrated waves of weird events?

Patterns in Time

Speculations on names and places are one intriguing aspect of Fortean thought; ideas about the patterns in time are another one. Let's look at some of the things people have had to say when they have ventured into this line of exploration.

In June of 1976, John Green, famed Sasquatch chronicler from British Columbia, fed 1,350 Sasquatch/Bigfoot reports into a computer in an attempt to get a portrait of these creatures and their behaviors. He was able to discover some composites, but, in general, he was frustrated by the effort. After discussing this in his book, *Sasquatch: The Apes Among Us*, he writes:

> Anyone trying seriously to make some sense out of this is probably fuming by now, because you obviously don't learn much unless you can relate things like time of day, time of year, type of location, geographic location, activity of the witness, etc., and find consistent patterns. If the weather, the altitude, and the phase of the moon would fit in too, that would be even better. That is the sort of thing we tried to do with the computer, and I have spent many a day at it with pencil and paper. I have made charts that will tell what the witness was doing, the type of locale, the season, the time of day, whether it was forested or open, what decade it was, approximately how high, in what state, whether there was snow on the ground, and whether there were tracks found, all from a single entry. I also have maps marked to show what was seen, what time of day, what time of year, by whom, how long ago, how high, and whether there was snow on the ground. They don't show any useful pattern at all. What they do show is that the patterns some people claim to have found — migration routes for instance — just aren't there.

With all that said, Green still was able to come up with some amazing general remarks about patterns. "The most common type of report in British Columbia is a Sasquatch seen on the beach from a boat in the daytime," Green observed. Looking at seasons, he found "the most common form of sighting is by someone driving on a side road, in the fall, in California or Washington." Green learned those things from the computer. But this man's sense of the phenomena are just as important. He writes:

> Actually the people with the best mathematical chance to see a Sasquatch are almost certainly those who sit up nights where skunk apes have been reported garbage hunting in western Florida, and after that would come anyone who regularly drives the road to Easterville in northern Manitoba—but I didn't learn those things from statistics.

Other Bigfoot researchers have had feelings about the patterns of the sightings, and sometimes they did involve the phases of the moon. Shortly before he died, George Haas, founder of the *Bigfoot Bibliography*, told me that he had strong evidence that most of the northern California encounters were occurring during the new moon. Some Bigfooters have related this to the "dark of the moon" hunting behavior of some larger animals; others don't know what it means. Green found that the earlier reports from before 1970 were mainly daytime sightings, but he had seen a drift in the southern California and eastern U.S.A. cases by the mid-seventies. "The vast majority are at night," Green wrote.

The Extremes of April and May

One anomaly John Green seems especially troubled with is the very low number of sightings during one particular month:

> The puzzling thing . . . is the low total for May, which is quite consistent geographically . . . . If there is a month when Sasquatches head for the high country or the deep bush, May is apparently it. Perhaps they are shy creatures and May is the mating season. I don't know anything on the human side of the situation to explain it. Possibly it is just accidental and will disappear when more reports are in, but it doesn't seem likely.

Interestingly, Green's May anomaly agrees with the evidence coming out of other monster cycles.

Analyzing all the phantom panther reports I had from the East for the years 1900 to 1970, I was struck by how they seemed to clump in the winter months of November, December, and January, and in the summer-fall ones of June, July, August, and September. August had the most number of sightings; May the least. Graphically speaking, May appeared to be in a valley between some very high frequencies for April and the beginning of the summer curve in June.

Then Gary Mangiacopra sent me his results for the Northeast's sea serpent sightings. Systematically searching through six daily newspapers for the years 1869 to 1976, Mangiacopra surveyed just over 640 years of news, page by page. A truly monumental effort. What he found tends to agree with what Green and I found. Mangiacopra noted: "Roughly three-fourths of all sightings were occurring during

(courtesy of the Institute of Fortean Studies)

Hyampom, California. In 1963 noted Sasquatch researcher John Green (far left) posed with Syl McCoy and Bruce Berryman, who had made these plaster casts of Bigfoot prints they had recently found. Green's decades of investigations have led him to some interesting conclusions on the nature of the patterns underlying the reports of Bigfoot/Sasquatch.

the summer months. The remaining one-fourth was occurring during the fall and winter months, during the time of which one would generally assume sightings would not be reported."

So what happened to spring sightings of the creatures? Before the turn of the century, Mangiacopra could not find one sea-serpent report for March, April, or May. During the entire period of his search, he discovered July, followed by August, were the high reporting months. Why are monsters seen less often in the late spring in North America, when, with more people coming outside to enjoy the warmer weather, you would expect more sightings?

As you may recall from chapter 1, Dr. Frederick Aldrich found a thirty-year cycle in the giant squid appearances off Newfoundland, with peaks in the 1870s, 1900 to 1910, 1930s, and 1960s. Gary Mangiacopra discovered a similar, if not fainter, cycle for North America sea serpent appearances in the late 1870s, late 1880s, mid-1890s, throughout the period from 1900 to 1910, again starting up in 1929 through the 1930s, and finally with a mini-wave in 1957 to 1964. Is there some relationship between Aldrich's and Mangiacopra's cycles? We also note, Aldrich says the giant squids are mostly seen and wash ashore in the autumn.

Even the thunderbirds, as I noted in chapter 3, tend to be seen on either side of May, with highs mainly for April and in the summer. Michael A. Persinger and Gyslaine F. Lafreniere also comment on this in their massive work on Fortean patterns, *Space-Time Transients and Unusual Events*. They found that: "Conspicuously, the unknown flying creature subcategory peaks in April for the years analyzed."

Out-of-place alligators, which I listed in *Mysterious America*, also show this dislike for May.

The Depth of the Cycles

Although you may be ready to dismiss this obvious lack of reports for May as some function of only mysterious animals (sea serpents, giant squids, phantom panthers, thunderbirds, erratic alligators, and Bigfeet) I would caution you to not form your opinions too swiftly. Something deeper seems to be going on here. All we have to do is turn to the field of ufology, the study of UFOs, to find some similarly unsettling statistics.

Looking at well over ten thousand reports of UFOs, John A. Keel came up with some startling findings and noted in his *UFOs-Operation Trojan Horse*:

> It is obvious that the phenomenon is controlled by hidden laws and cycles. Psychic and occult events seem to follow the same cycles as the UFO phenomenon. The Wednesday-Saturday phenomenon exists in all the frames of reference. For some reason, the twenty-fourth days of

> April, June, September, November, and December seem to produce exceptional activity year after year . . . .
> . . . These events are staged year after year, century after century, in the same exact areas and often on the same exact calendar dates. Only the witnesses and the frames of reference used are different.

Commenting on the mysterious timetable on which the phenomenon appears to be working, Keel comments further on the exact periods and places of probable contact:

> So if you are eager to see a genuine example of our phenomenon, pick a good Wednesday or Saturday evening, visit the highest ground in the area closest to you which has a magnetic fault, and watch the sky around 10:00 P.M. The best times are the last two weeks in March and the first two weeks in April, all of July-August, the last two weeks in October, and the first weeks in November and December.

Needless to say, you might want to check behind you for a phantom panther or a ghost, if you find yourself on the keel of a hill merely watching the skies waiting for a UFO. I suspect these guidelines cross all kinds of phenomena.

Others have suggested as much. Damon Knight tells of how, while doing research for his book on Charles Fort, he typed twelve hundred file cards containing all the dates and data from Fort's books. What Knight found, for example, for the years 1877 to 1892, was that reports of storms, falls, and things seen in space and in the skies all peaked in the same years.

Persinger and Lafreniere, who developed a theory of geomagnetic interaction and correlationship to Fortean phenomena, fill their book with graphs that have trends similar to those seen by Green, Mangiacopra, Keel, and myself. They show, for instance, that spontaneous human combustions appear to peak in the winter and during April. Forteans have discovered that across the board the time cycles keep showing up. Late in April 1985, for example, starfish fell from the sky onto lawns in St. Cloud, Minnesota.

A Special Day

While the whole "hot" month of April, filled with everything from last century's reports of airships and phantom trains to the recent accounts of flying men and giant birds, tends to be important, in terms of intrigue, one of the most long-lasting cycles has been that associated with a specific date—24 June.

June twenty-fourth is St. John's Day. The feast of St. John the Baptist is one of the oldest, if not the oldest, to be introduced into the liturgies of the Greek and Latin churches in a saint's honor. Instead of the customary way of celebrating a saint's day on the day of his death, this day is remembered for St. John's birth. St. John is invoked against hail (please note, falling ice), epilepsy, convulsion, and spasms.

(The man himself, John the Baptist, is seen as the forerunner, cousin, and baptizer of Jesus. Living in the wilderness, he is portrayed as a mystic who lived on a diet of locusts and wild honey [see Matthew 3]. His beheading is frequently depicted in Christian art.)

St. John's Day was long associated in Europe with the midsummer festivities. On St. John's Eve fires were built on every hill, a survival of the old custom of lighting Beltane fires, dedicated to the god Bel or Baal. (Although "Beltane," per se, is 1 May, the fires lit at all lunar and solar festivals are often referred to as "Beltane fires.")

The Irish and English used to believe that on St. John's Eve the soul of every person left their body, found the place where they would die, and then returned to the body. A person sitting on a church porch all night fasting would see passing before him all the local people who would die during the coming year. In many ways, these traditions are akin to those at Halloween in which the souls of the dead circulate in graveyards.

As the Bords note in their excellent book, *Earth Rites*, St. John's Day/ Midsummer Day is associated with dancing around a birch tree in a fashion not unlike the fertility rites of dancing about the maypole on May Day. They observe that the tree in one way is the earth phallus, "the male principle jutting out of the earth," while on the other it is like a "fruit-bearing tree of life," which is female.

Fairies, the Occult and 24 June

The pagan custom of bathing and round dances on St. John's Eve was forbidden by the church in an effort to stamp out all past fertility rites. Likewise the collecting of the glowworms and the luminous St. John's wort occurred through the night beginning on St. John's Eve. The

(courtesy of the Institute of Fortean Studies from a painting by Andrea del Sarto in the Pitti Palace, Florence, Italy)

John the Baptist. A mystic who lived in the wilderness, and ate locusts and honey, John the Baptist's birth date on 24 June has taken on special importance in attempts to understand the cycles of unexplained phenomena.

wort was seen as equal protection against the devil and from abduction by fairies. ("Pagan" is a word with origins in the movement to dismiss earth rites' impact and import in everyday living. Pagan merely means "rural folk.")

Obviously, the rural festivals marking the summer solstice and midsummer's day had to be dealt with by the church, and St. John's Day was created. However, the wonder of this special time, acknowledged by these past peoples so deeply in tune with Gaia, has not been so easily diminished.

Elizabethan England felt the date was important as a time when fairies and the little people were around and about. Shakespeare's *A Midsummer Night's Dream*, with its rich lore of the fairy, Puck, or Robin Goodfellow, is familiar to many, but few nowadays recall its relationship to 24 June.

Adepts in the occult have long been aware of the significance of the day, and have used the "power" of the date to conjure new ventures. Edward III, king of England, as a great follower of the legendary King Arthur and the Round Table, founded The Order of the Garter on 24 June 1348. In 1633 on 24 June the Inquisition released Galileo. In 1717, the Grand Lodge of Freemasons was inaugurated in London. By tradition this is the date in the thirteenth century that the Pied Piper of Hamelin returned, piped his haunting tune, and captivated 130 children into following him from town to a mountain, never to be seen again. This was, literally, an enchanted kidnapping on a grand scale.

An early American utopian community known as the "Woman of the Wilderness" was entwined with St. John's Day. Sailing from Germany on 13 February 1694, they arrived at their destination, Germantown, Pennsylvania on 24 June of the same year, and immediately burned St. John's bonfires, made ritual incantations, and called on heavenly powers to sanctify their new home. The group was an interesting mixture of believers in Primitive Christianity, Theosophy, Rosiscrucianism, and paganism; were energetic musicians and active educators; and were responsible for the first volume of music published in America.

During the seventh anniversary of the Woman of the Wilderness' arrival, a curious incident occurred of particular connection to the matters under examination. According to Mark Holloway's *Heavens on Earth*, just as members of the community were about to light their bonfire, "a white, obscure, moving body in the air attracted their attention, which, as it approached, assumed the form and mien of an angel. It receded into the shadows of the forest and appeared again immediately before them as the fairest of the lovely." Holloway notes they fell to their knees and prayed but "their angel vanished, without so much as a word of good cheer." This encounter overlaps with many accounts we have studied of UFOs, religious visions, and angelic ufonauts (please see my first book, *The Unidentified*) and significantly took place on 24 June 1701.

More recently, investigators of the unexplained have sensed something was different about this date. Charles Fort wrote of a mysterious jelly-like mass that was found covering the ground at Eton, Bucks, England in 1911 on June twenty-fourth. And in true Fortean fashion there are a couple of falls for 1877: a red rain fell on parts of Italy on St. John's Eve, and then huge pieces of ice dropped from the sky at Fort Lyon, Colorado on 24 June.

Even bizarre disappearances focus on this date. According to the Soviet newspaper *Pravda*, a freight train, with twenty-eight cars carrying crushed rocks, left the Tomashgrodsky, U.S.S.R. factory on 24 June 1983, never to be seen again. As the Russian press commented: "It left, but it never arrived."

The Significance of 24 June 1947

No one will need to remind ufologists of the critical importance of this date. On 24 June 1947 the modern era of UFOs began with Kenneth Arnold's dramatic sighting of "saucers" flying between Mount Rainier and Mount Adams in Washington. Because of the primary significance of this particular date, however, searching more broadly into other events occurring on that day appears to reveal some hidden connections to St. John's Day.

The headline news event for 24 June 1947 (obviously published in the next day's papers) was the beginning of a massive coal miner's strike in the U.S.A. (Coal-men, of course, have always been associated, traditionally, with the burning of the Beltane and beacon fires of old, along ley lines. UFOs, literally "fires in the skies," some writers believe, "travel" the ley lines.) We find the news of 24 June 1947 filled with reports of fires. A large fire in Brussels killed seventeen when a stock of film mysteriously and spontaneously exploded and trapped five hundred people, for a time, in a building. A huge fire in Perth Amboy, New Jersey destroyed a department store and caused the evacuation of two adjoining movie theaters. A big fire was reported in London. A United Air Lines plane traveling from Chicago to Cleveland was struck and burned by a bolt of lightning. Fire equipment waited on the ground just in case the plane crashed; it landed safely.

In a bizarre twist of fate, since St. John's Day is named after a man who ate locusts and wild honey, we note that on 24 June 1947 the nations of Guatemala and El Salvador were said to be using fire in the form of flame-throwers to destroy hordes of grasshoppers invading their countries. Meanwhile, back in Washington, where Kenneth Arnold was experiencing and telling about a UFO sighting that would soon greatly influence the future, a Katherine Moseley of Seattle was being stung to death by wasps or bees. (Perhaps the name game is at play here too, as the years since 1947 have seen a James Moseley become one of the foremost figures in ufology. Moseley's personal and folksy style has made his name a buzz-word in the field. He is viewed as an appealing and popular figure among hundreds of flying saucer buffs, and he annually receives national recognition awards in huge meetings ignored by the media.)

Other UFO Connections of St. John's Day

Otto Binder and John Keel have noticed a number of "seeming coincidental deaths in the UFO field on 24 June," including in 1964 Frank Scully, author of one of the first crashed-saucer books; contactee Arthur Bryant in 1967; British contactee Richard Church also in 1967; and Willy Ley in 1969. Frank Edwards, popular UFO author and radio personality in the 1950s, died a few hours before Bryant.

June twenty-fourths have had their share of weird UFO accounts since 1947, as well. For example, in 1953 a gigantic UFO with a series of red lights and portholes was seen over Hampton Bay, Long Island. While it flew backwards over water, it made "the same noise as a swarm of bees!" Two days later a "yellowish moss" was found at the site. The connections between the elements of this report and the bees/honey of St. John seem quite obvious. As Jerry Clark and I stated in our 1975 book, *The Unidentified*, many fairy witnesses hear the sound of buzzing flies or bees. Speaking of UFOs, we wrote:

"Contactees occasionally remark on the 'bee-buzzing' sound at the beginning and/or conclusion of their encounters." In Orphic tradition, the bee had a deep spiritual importance. Human souls were said to travel in swarms, like swarms of bees. The grasshopper or locust, likewise, travels in swarms and has had symbolic significance in ancient times; for example, the golden locust is the emblem of the sun-god Apollo.

Swarms of unidentified flying objects and this specific day have a long-shared history that continues to the present. As the Associated Press noted for 24 June 1985: "Over northern and central Florida, a string of bright lights sweeping accross the sky Monday night prompted thousands of phone calls from people alarmed about UFOs."

Furthermore, ambrosia, the thick, syrupy, honey-like food of the gods, fairies, and little people, often given to mortal men, shares traits with these stories. Ambrosia, in more modern times, appears to have turned up as the Long Island yellowish moss of 24 June 1953, the jelly masses found at Eton on 24 June 1911, and the traditional 24 June yellow St. John's wort so often associated with protection from the fairies. (Fairy abductions and UFO kidnappings are merely different guises of the same phenomenon.)

And Monsters Too

But besides UFO-related stories, strange monster accounts have turned up on St. John's Day as well. A couple of examples demonstrates the bizarre nature of the cases. In the midst of a series of winged vampire cat incidents in Ontario, on 24 June 1966, one of these critters was apparently pumped full of bullets in the village of Alfred. A flap of Bigfoot-like creature sightings in Logan and Union Counties, Ohio took place in 1980, but the Bords note:

> The *strangest* [emphasis added] was the encounter reported by Union County legal secretary Mrs. Donna Riegler. She was driving home from work on 24 June. It was a stormy evening after a hot, muggy day. Lightning flickered, the sky darkened, and large drops of rain began to fall, but Mrs. Riegler had no inkling of what was about to happen. She told a reporter: "I was in a good mood. I just wanted to get home. I went over the railroad tracks slow. I always do because I don't want to knock

my wheels out of line. Then I saw this thing laying on the road, hunched over. I thought it was a dog at first. Then it stood up, and I thought it was a man. I thought he was crazy, laying on the road. I couldn't figure why he was out there. He had no golf clubs. No luggage. Then he turned around and looked at me." When asked for more details of the creature's appearance, she demonstrated its posture: upright, with knees bent, and hands held out, palms up. She could not see any facial features. Mrs. Riegler escaped as fast as she could, stopping at a stranger's house where, unnerved by her experience, she broke down and sobbed.

Gaia's Patterns and Fortean Insights

We shall pick up an existence by its frogs.—Charles Fort

Stepping back from it all, we realize there are no real answers to the phenomena. But perhaps, by continuing to look at the underlying patterns we can begin to see the whole elephant, the organism that is Gaia. She apparently has disturbances that might be earthquakes, or ice falls, or fires in the skies. She apparently has cycles or periods of outbursts of electromagnetic energies, monsters, and poltergeists. And she even has dates and months that we humans have tried to fit within our context of understanding with festivals and flaps, on which she remembers something and acts upon it. Our existence is an organism, and we think we can know our existence not just by frogs, as Fort stated, but by its bees, as well.

The Lists

A procession of the damned. By the damned, I mean the excluded. We shall have a procession of data that Science has excluded. —Charles Fort

Appendix I
Ghosts on the Tracks: Phantom Trains, Spook Lights, and Other Rail Phenomena

The following list details known locations, by state/province, city, and railroad, if known, of all phantom trains for North America. Specific descriptions of the nature of the phantom train reports are given.

For spook lights, ghostly lanterns, and hauntings associated with railroads, the state/province, city, and rail line are inventoried. Please refer to the more complete list of spook lights in my previous book, *Mysterious America*, for other such sites.

Ghosts on the Tracks: Phantom Trains, Spook Lights, and Other Rail Phenomena

United States—Phantom Trains

Arizona
Wilcox: Alkali Flats/light, smoke, ghost train, engineer

Colorado
Marshall Pass: Union Pacific Railroad/see chapter 7

Connecticut
Falls Village: Housatonic Railroad/see chapter 7

Florida
Bartow: Railroad/whistles

Georgia
McDonough/Railroad/whistles, engine noises, steam

Kansas
Edwardsville: Kansas Pacific Railroad/see chapter 7

Massachusetts

Pittsfield: Pittsfield and North Adams Railroad/see *Mysterious America*

Woburn: Boston and Lowell Railroad/light, engine, ghost train

Minnesota

Baudette: Railroad/ghost train

New Jersey

Newark: New Jersey Central Railroad/whistles

New York

Albany: New York Central Railroad/"Lincoln's funeral train"/see chapter 7

North Carolina

Statesville: Atlantic Coast Line Railroad/whistles, light, coaches, wreck

Warsaw: Atlantic Coast Line Railroad/whistles, lights, cars, steam, wreck

Ohio

Shelby: Yazoo and Mississippi Valley Railroad/"engine working steam"

Virginia

Staunton: Railroad/ghost train

Washington

Eagle Gorge: Burlington Northern Railroad/ghost "Locomotive #33"

Canada—Phantom Trains

Nova Scotia

Cape Breton/Barrachois: Nova Scotia Railroad/ghost train

United States—Locations of R.R. Spook Lights and Phantom Lantern Tales

Arkansas

Crossett: Missouri-Pacific Railroad

Gurdon: Missouri-Pacific Railroad

California

Berkeley: Bay Area Rapid Transit (BART)/under University and Shattuck Aves.

Georgia

Macon: Railroad

Indiana
Danville: Railroad Bridge/White Lick Creek

Massachusetts
North Adams: Troy and Greenfield Railroad/Hoosac Tunnel
Raynham: Railroad

Mississippi
Artesia: Railroad track

Missouri
Matthews: Cotton Belt Railroad

New Jersey
Flanders: Central Railroad of New Jersey
Long Valley: High Bridge Railroad
Mt. Olive: Central Railroad of New Jersey
Washington Township

North Carolina
Chapel Hill: Louisville and Nashville Railroad
Jamestown: Southern Railroad Overpass
Maco: Atlantic Coast Line Railroad Trestle/Hood's Creek
Wrightsville: Southern Railroad

Ohio
Arcadia: Lake Erie & Western Railroad
Lake Hope: Railroad and Moonville tunnel
Toledo: Baltimore and Ohio Railroad

Pennsylvania
Jordan's Valley: Reading Railroad House
Newport: Erie Railroad Bridge

Texas
Lufkin: Southern Pacific Railroad
Marfa: Southern Pacific Railroad
Saratoga: Old Santa Fe Railroad Bed/dirt road

Vermont
Essex Junction: Central Vermont Railroad

Virginia
Suffolk: Old Jackson and Whaleyville Railroad Bed/Jackson Road

West Virginia
Cottageville: Baltimore & Ohio Railroad

Wisconsin
Eagle River: Old Railroad Bed/Dog Meadow

Appendix II
Spooky Sites: Haunted and
Ghostly Locations of North America

I have attempted to gather together all the material and notes I could find on every place in the United States of America and Canada that I know is spooky, with some notable exceptions: I did not include the devil-named sites, Lafayette locations, and spook lights spots already listed in *Mysterious America* (please refer to chapters 3, 21, and 23 and to appendix I for these localities). Likewise, the spook light spots noted previously in appendix I of this book are worthy of your inspection.

Spooky Sites: Haunted and Ghostly Locations of North America

United States of America

Alabama

Battles Wharf
Birmingham: Bayview Bridge
Cahaba: Saltmarsh Hall
Courtland: Rocky Hill Castle
Demopolis: Gaineswood
Furman: Savage Hill
Kinston: Harrison Cemetery
Marion: Carlisle Hall
Mobile
  Bienville Square
  Madison Manor
  Toulmin House
Montgomery: Pratt Hall/Huntington College
Prattville: Gurney Manufacturing Factory
Prichard: Bliunt High School

Selma: Sturdivant Hall
Tuscaloosa
Old Drish Plantation Home
Smith Hall Museum, University of Alabama

Alaska
Sitka: Baranof Castle

Arizona
Cerbat Mountains
Douglas: Gadsden Hotel
Kingman: Death Trap Mountain
Phoenix: Indian School Road
Superstition Mountains
Tinajas Altas Spring: Laguna Prieta and Mission of the Four Evangelists
Tucson
Old El Cerro Colorado Mine
Stone Avenue Underpass

Arkansas
Arkadelphia: Barkman House
Clarksville: College of the Ozarks
Fayetteville: Lake Wedington
Fort Smith
Jailhouse
Rector Heights
Helena: 404 College Street
Ozark Mountains
Pine Bluff: Sawdust Bridge
Tucker: Prison Farm

California
Aetna Springs: Resort
Alabama Hills
Anza Borrego Desert
Bel-Air: Pink (Mansfield) House
Berkeley
Faculty Club, University of California
Siegal Rock

Beverly Hills
  Elke Sommer's Benedict Canyon Home
  2320 Bowman Drive
Big Bear City: Rebel Ridge
Bodega: Charlene's Yesterday Museum
Bodie: Graveyard
Breckenridge Mountain
Bridgeport: Poor Farm
Camarillo: State Hospital
Chino
Clayton
  Ingram Cave
  Live Oak Cemetery
  Morgan Territory Road
  Town Hall
Cobblestone Mountain
Coloma: Vineyard House
Coulterville: Highway 32
Fair Oaks: American River/Sailor's Bar
Fountain Valley: Stowe House
Fresno
  1818 Tyler Street
  St. John's Cathedral
Funeral Mountains
Gardena: Airport
Georgetown: Elliott Home
Green Lake
Hillsborough: 85 Country Club Drive
Hollywood: Houdini Mansion grounds
Irvine Beach: Peters Canyon Road
Kelso Valley: Sheep Springs
Kennedy Meadow: Nine-Mile Canyon
Laguna Beach: Hangover House
Lake Tahoe
Little Lake
Los Angeles
  Ardmore Blvd
  City Hall

Eagle Rock
Hillcrest Church
96th Street
Petit Street
337 S. Main Street
Valentino's Movie Studio
Lynwood: Lago Avenue
Mare Island: Naval Reserve
Mill Valley: Tiburon Point Castle
Misery Mountain
Monterey: Casa Bodega Liquor Store
Monterey: Robert Lewis Stevenson's Houston Street House
Mount Shasta
Mount Tamalpais
North Hollywood: Riverside Drive
Oakland Hills: Slaughter Hunting Lodge
Oakland: 1904 Franklin Street
Ojai: Creek Road
Orange County
Black Star Canyon/Irvine Mansion
El Toro Cemetery
Knott's Berry Farm
Mission San Juan Capistrano
Peters Canyon
Santa Ana Canyon
Silverado Canyon
Trabuco Creek
Yorba Linda Cemetery
Palo Alto: 500 Block Emerson Street
Pigeon Point: Coast Guard Lighthouse
Pomona: Casa Alvarado
Sacramento: 5848 14th Avenue
Saint Helena: Spring Hill Farm
San Diego
Navy Electronic Lab/Loma Portal
Whaley House
San Francisco
Alcatraz

Bank of America
Bush and Octavia Street
California Street near Fairmont Hotel
Lombard Street
Russian Hill
Sutro's Baths
Toravel Street
2544 Clement Avenue
2221 Washington Street
San Jose
LeBaron Hotel/Room 538
Sarah Winchester Mystery House
San Simeon: Hearst Castle
Santa Cruz Mountains
Smith Valley
Sonoma
Blue Wing Inn
Wolf House
Stockton: Rose Street
Sunnyvale: Toys-R-Us Store
Tehachapi Mountains
Thousand Oaks
Missionary Baptist Church
Stagecoach Inn
Tustin: Pacific Street
Valley of the Moon
Ventura
Meta Street
Mission San Buenaventura
Ventura Theater
Wheeler Canyon
Yerba Buena Island: Lighthouse
Yucaipa: 33843 Fairview Road

Colorado

Arena Creek
Deadman Creek
Denver
Bradmar House

- 4100 S. University Avenue
- 2334 Lawrence Street

Dory Hill
Greeley: Poudre River
Hall Valley
Jamestown: Quartz Mine
Pike's Peak
Westminster: Andrews House

Connecticut

Bridgeport: Lindley Street
Cornwall
- Dark Entry Ravine
- Dudleytown

East Hartford: Hockanum Caseway
Greenwich: St. Paul's Episcopal Church
Groton Long Point
Hanging Hills
Milldale: West Peak
Moodus: Mount Tom
Mount Riga
New Haven: Woolsley Hall, Yale University
North Woodstock: Brickyard Road
Norwich: Spite House
Stratford: Phelps House
Talcott Mountains
West Hartford: Reservoir
Windham: Frog Pond

Delaware

Brandywine: Riverview Cemetery
Dover
- King George III Inn
- Woodburn (Governor's) Mansion

Newark: Brookside

District of Columbia

Capitol Building
Decatur House
Ford's Theater
Fort McNair

Halcyon House
Lincoln Memorial
National Theater
Navy Yard
Octagon
Pentagon
Petersen House
Tingey House
White House
Woodrow Wilson House

Florida

Cayo Pelau
Coral Gables: Miami Biltmore Hotel
Defuniak Springs: Eden State Garden
Fort George Island: Kingsley Plantation
Key West: Audubon House
Miami
  Laubheim Warehouse
  Tropication Arts
  22nd Avenue and 28th Street
Oklawaha: Bradford House
Tallahassee: Department of Corrections Building
Wakulla Springs
West Palm Beach: La Petite Poodle
Winter Springs: Turner Home

Georgia

Adel: No Man's Friend Pond
Atlanta
  Fort McPherson
  Oakland Cemetery
  St. Michael's Church
Columbus: Springer Opera House
Dale: Telegraph Tower
Kinchafoonee Creek
Oakville: Old Walsingham House
Plains: Old Carter House
Riverside: Fort Benning
Saint Simon's Island

Christ Church
Ebo Landing
Whitmire Hill

Hawaii

Ewa: 91-1668 Pahiki Street
Honolulu: Hawaiian Village Hilton
Kawela Bay
Kohala Mountains
Mauna Loa: Ka-upe
Nuuana Valley
Old Waimea: Firehouse
Waiane: 85-904 Imipono Street

Idaho

McCammon: I-15, between mileposts 47 and 57

Illinois

Alsip: Cemetery at 115th Street
Bartonville: State Hospital Cemetery
Belleville: Main and 17th Street
Chicago
Biograph Theater
Clark Street near Lincoln Park
Holy Family Church
Hull House
Hyde Park
Irish Castle
Kaiser Hall
Kedzie Avenue
Knights of Columbus at 33rd Street
St. Rita's Church
3375 Oakley Avenue
Crestwood: Bachelor Grove Cemetery
Cumberland County: Embarrass River
Edwardsville: R.C. Scheffel and Company
Equality: Old Slave House
Jonesboro: Dug Hill
Justice: Resurrection Cemetery
Lawrenceville: High School
Macomb: Charles Willey Farm

Mason: Little Wabash River Bridge
McLeansboro: Lakey's Creek
Oak Lawn: Holy Sepulchre Cemetery
Oakley: Peck Cemetery
Springfield
  Lincoln Home
  Oak Ridge Cemetery
  Old Courthouse
Tunnel Hill: Skunk Hollow
Urbana
  Urbana High School tower
  Woodlawn Cemetery
  Ursa: Old Covered Bridge
  Voorhies: Voorhies Castle
  Woodstock: Opera House

Indiana
Benton: Rising Sun Cemetery
Decatur County: Sand Creek
Dublin: Cry Woman Bridge
Indianapolis
  Hannah House
  2910 West Delaware Street
Lafayette
Lake Manitou
Notre Dame: Washington Hall
Osceola: Greenlawn Avenue

Iowa
Columbus Junction
Davenport: Pi Kappa Chi Fraternity
Dubuque: Ham House
Iowa City: Sumter House
Millville: Split-Level Road
Mount Pleasant
Spirit Canyon

Kansas
Clay County: Jesse James Homestead
Doniphan: Doniphan Lake
Fort Riley: George Custer House

Lawrence: Old Delaware Mills
Manhattan: Manhattan Avenue
Oak Canyon
Sterling: Broadway Station

Kentucky

Bardstown: Nelson County Jail
Blue Mountains
Brandenburg: Woodland
Dunnville: Old Bailey House
Frankfort: Liberty Hall
Louisville
  Camp Taylor
  Fern Creek
  Stuckenberg Place
Mulberry Hill
Owensboro: Wilson's Ferry
Pikeville: Chloe Creek Mine

Louisiana

Baton Rouge
  The Cottage Plantation
  Skolfield House
Bayou Grand Sara: Moonrise Plantation
Estopinal: Kenilworth Plantation
Franklin: Oaklawn Manor
Hahnville: Vie Fortune Plantation
Lake Pontchartrain
Marksville: Forest
Monroe: Limerick Plantation
Natchitoches
  Lacey Branch
  Simmons House
New Orleans
  Beauregard (Le Carpentier) House
  Carrollton Jail
  Cherokee Street
  Delphine La Laurie Mansion
  1813 St. Anthony Street
  1447 Constance Street
  Fourth Street
  Gardette-Le Pretre Mansion

Governor Nichols Street
Lafayette Cemetery
Laveau House
St. Ann and Royal Street
St. Louis Cemetery No. 1
Seaman's Bethel
Treme Street Bridge
Tulane and Saratoga Street Jail
2606 Royal Street
New Roads: Parlange Plantation
Saint Bernard: Mercier Plantation
Saint Francisville: The Myrtles Plantation
Saint Maurice: St. Maurice Plantation
Vacherie: Valcour Aime Plantation Gardens
Vidalia: Jailhouse

Maine

Alfred: Owl Tree
Benton Falls: Linnell Home
Bridgton: Sweden/Burnham School Road
Brooklin: Cooper Home
Bucksport: Cemetery
Cochnewagan Pond
Damariscotta: Mary Howe House
Darkharbor
Deer Point: Peabody House
Douglas Hill
Duck Neck: Medomak River Point
Dungarvon River
Fayette: Jolly Hollow
Freeport: Old Means Tavern Site
Hallowell: Town Roads
Hollis Center: Sawmill
Johnson's Bay: Pirate's Creek
Jonesboro: Hilton's Neck
Kennebunk: Kennebeck Inn
Kennebunkport: Morgan House
Machaisport: Old Blaisdel House
Matinicus Rock: Lighthouse
New Gloucester: Route 26/Shaker's Village
Newfield: Old Straw Place

- Pickering Island
- Pond Island
- Portland
  - Casco Bay
    - Marshall Island
    - Swan's Island
  - Serenity Hill
- Pownal: Oleson House
- Vinalhaven
- Wells: Haunted Valley
- Wiscassett
  - Lee Payson Smith House
  - Marine Antique Shop
  - Musical Wonder House
- Woolrich
  - Burnt Hill
  - Hockomock Point

Maryland

- Annapolis
  - Chandler Mansion
  - 42 East Street
  - West Point
  - Baltimore
    - Fayette Street Westminster Presbyterian Churchyard
    - 1448 Meridene Drive
    - Hampton Mansion
    - Locust Point
    - USF Constellation
  - Boonesboro: South Mountain
  - Church Creek
  - Clinton: Surratt Tavern
  - Crisfield
    - Asbury Church Cemetery
    - Horsey Place
  - Emmitsburg: Cemetery
  - Fort Howard: Todd House
  - Golden Hill: Catholic Church
  - Gum Briar Swamp

- Indian Head
- Oyster Point
- Port Tobacco: Rose Hill
- Smith Island
- Towson: Hampton National Historic Site
- Warfieldburg: Ore Mine Bridge
- Westminster
  - Leigh Master Estate
  - Maryland Hunt Cup Course

Massachusetts

- Amesbury: Barrow Hill
- Ashland: John Stone's Inn
- Athol
  - Crescent Street Bridge
  - Sanders Street
  - Silver Lake
- Barnstable: Public Housing Authority
- Bish-Bash Falls State Park: Bish-Bash Falls
- Boston
  - 1 Arlington Street
  - 1 Garrett Street
  - Boston Harbor Islands
    - Apple Island
    - Clark's Island
    - George's Island: Fort Warren
    - Long Island
  - Cedar Grove Cemetery
  - King's Lane
  - Logan Airport
- Bridgewater: Hockomock Swamp
- Cambridge
  - The Commons
  - Riedesel Mansion
- Charlton: Massachusetts Turnpike Information Center
- Cohasset: Ship's Chandlery
- Danvers: Gallows Hills
- Dighton: Colonel Richmond House
- Douglas: Orchard

Dover: Polka Rock
Great Barrington: Three Mile Hill
Hadley
  Elm Valley
  Huntington House
  Wilder Hall, Mount Holyoke College
Halifax: Davis Farm
Haverhill: Buttonwoods Museum
Hingham: Eastgate Lane
Hopkinton: 86 Elm Street
Ipswich: Congregational Church
Lake Quannapowette
Lawrence: 26 Florence Street
Lowell: Christian Hill
Lynn: Lynn Woods Reservation/Dungeon Rock
Malden: Cemetery
Marblehead
  Oakum Bay
  Screeching Lady Beach
Marshfield: Phillips Mansion
Medford: Rock Hill Estate
Medway: Dinglehole
Methuen: 1 Linton Avenue
Milton: Milton Hill
Newburyport: 32 Charles Street
Plum Island
Quincy: St. Mary's Cemetery
Salem: Joshua Ward House
Somerville: Washington Street
Springfield
  Hotel
  7 Butler Street
Warren: Waternomee Falls
Wellesley: Golf Course
Woburn
  Black House
  Central House
  Dunham's Pond
  First Baptist Church

Horn Pond
Wright's Pond

Michigan
Caribou Island
Detroit
5508 Martin Street
Howard and 19th Street
Nain Rouge
Dixboro
Frankfort: LaRue Home
Grand Rapids
Prospect Avenue SE
Sanford Mansion
Grand Sable Banks
Grosse Pointe Park
Hamtramck: 9485 Mitchell Street
Holland: Lodge Post
Holly: Robinson Home
Lansing: St. Joseph Cemetery
Lapeer: Calhoun Street
McBain: McBain House
Munising: West Superior Street
Stambaugh: Riverton Mine
Westland: Butler Cemetery

Minnesota
Canby
Collegeville: St. John's Abbey
Crookston
Eagle Lake
Gibbon
Hastings
Lake Park
Minneapolis
Chelberg House
City Hall
Guthrie Theater
Owatonna
Russell

St. Paul
  Forepaugh's
  476 Summit Avenue
  Griggs House
Silver Lake
Vondell Brooks

Mississippi
Beauregard: E.A. Rowan House
Gulfport: Cahill House
Natchez
  Cottage Gardens
  Glenburnie House
  King's Tavern
  Longwood Plantation
Raleigh: Town Cemetery
Sunmer: Boone Jerkins House
Tupelo: Natchez Trace Parkway/Witch Dance

Missouri
Back Creek: Highway 61
Bolvair: Highway 13
Boonville: Muir Mansion
Breadtray Mountain
Cape Girardeau: Lorimer Cemetery
Cassville: Moaning Mountain
Everton: Old Payne Orchard
Fayette: Lilac Hill
Flat River: Red Onion Cave
Galena: Old McCord Farm
Hannibal: Bear Creek Cemetery
Kansas City: Emerson House, University of Missouri
Laddonia: Harbison Dairy Farm
Lake of the Ozarks: Glaize Park
Louisiana: River Road
Reeds Springs: Ghost Pond
Saint Genevieve: 1 North Street
Saint Joseph: Pacific House
Saint Louis
  Calvary Drive
  Clarion Hotel

Webster Groves
White River: Highway 13

Montana
Butte: Orphan Girl Mine
Missoula: South Fifth Street

Nebraska
Blackbird Hill
Lincoln: White Building, Nebraska Wesleyan University
Norfolk
110 Michigan
125 E. Park
Omaha: Court House

Nevada
Black Rock Range
Virginia City: Mary Louise Hospital

New Hampshire
Appledore Island: Babb's Cove
Chelsea: Orange County Jail
Derry: Beaver Lake
Hampton: Moulton House
Henniker: Ocean-Born Mary House
Isles of Shoals
Lancaster: Farrar House
Pittsfield: Ehrhardt Home
Sawyer's River
Troy
White Island
Woodsville: Lumber Mill

New Jersey
Atlantic City: Fire Engine Company No. 3
Barnegat Bay
Camden: 522 North Fifth Street
Cranbury: Truxton House
Jersey City: Wild Goose Tavern
Keansburg: St. Ann's Catholic Church
Mickleton: Bodo Otto House
Middletown: Spy House

Montclair: Rooming House
Morristown: Wedgewood Inn
Mount Holly
  Fair Haven
  Foy Homestead
Pompton Lakes: Sunnybank
Saddle River: Ringwood Manor
Schooley's Mountain
Scotch Plains
Shark River: Money Hill
Vincentown: Granite Castle
Winfield: 2-C Wavecrest Avenue

New Mexico

Alamogordo: 1712 Van Court
Carlsbad: Pecos River/Seep Canyon
Prewitt: Apache Burial Grounds
Taos: Dennis Hopper Hacienda

New York

Albany
  Graceland Cemetery
  Parsonage
Berne: Simmons Factory
Biddle Hollow
Binghamton: Vestal Home
Boytonville: State Route 7
Cherry Valley: Old Randall Place
Cincinnatus: Chenango Quarry
Cooperstown: River Street
Cortland: Joe Charles Sports Shop
Croton-On-Hudson: Van Cortlandt Manor House
Dosoris Island
Dunderberg
East Northport: 3 Purdy Avenue
Fort Johnson
Fredonia: State University College Building
Glen Cove: Morgan Hall
Greenwich: St. Paul's Episcopal Rectory
Hydesville: Fox Homestead
Irvington: Ardsley-On-Hudson

Kinderhook: Lindenwald
Livingston: Widow Mary's Place
Long Island: Mount Misery
Mamaroneck: Seven Oaks
Mohawk: Gelston Castle
Mount Van Hoevenberg
New York City
Atlantic Bridge
Austen House
Bayswater Road
Bergen House
Cafe Bizarre
Central Park
Church of St. Bartholomew
Clinton Court
Conference House
Crawley House
Dakota Apartments
Division Avenue
8th Avenue
84 Guernsey Street
Ellis Island
11 Bank Street
Empire Theater
51 West 10th Street
52 Willoughby Street
471 Central Park West
44th Street and 9th Avenue
Henderson Avenue
Hotel des Artistes
Howard Beach
John Jay House
Metropolitan Opera
Morris-Jumel Mansion
Old Merchant's House
Park Avenue
Riverside Drive
Riverside Museum
Rodenberg House
Roosevelt Avenue Station

1780 House/Stamford Hill
St. Mark's-in-the-Bowery Church
Shubert Alley
Snyder Avenue
1096 Lafayette Avenue
10th Street
34th Street and 3rd Avenue
Tillary and Concord Street
12 Gay Street
21st Street
27 Jane Street
226 West Fifth Avenue
West 87th Street
West 57th Street
West 56th Street
West 45th Street
West 12th Street
Women's Detention Prison
Nine Cornered Lake
Onondaga: Moor
Oswego: Fort Ontario
Pitcher Springs: Crofton Campsite/Otselic Valley
Poughkeepsie: Christ Church Rectory
Ramapo River
Rochester: Hawley Street
Rye
Barberry Lane
The Cedars
Sackets Harbor: Samuel Guthrie Home
Sag Harbor
Salem: Schoolhouse
Schenectady: Ellis Hospital Elevator B-1
Seaford: 1648 Redwood Path
Shelter Island
South Gilboa: Spook Woods
Syracuse: Syracuse Area Landmark Theatre
Tarrytown: Van Alen House
Ticonderoga: Fort Ticonderoga

Waterford: St. Mary's Church
Watkins Glen State Park
Wellsville: Pink House
West Point: Military Academy, Room 4714
Woodstock
Youngstown: Old Fort Niagara

North Carolina

Ashboro: Morrow Mountain
Asheville
  Royal Mountain
  Starnes Avenue
Balsam Mountains
Cape Fear River
Charlotte
  Great Gray Barn
  South Park Shopping Center
Cleveland County: Kadesh Church
Dallas: Old Jailhouse
Dunn: 809 E. Harnett
Eldorado: Old Coggins Gold Mine
Epsom: Neal Farm
Fayetteville: A.S. Slocumb House
French Broad River
Grandfather Mountain: Sawmill
Green Hill: Haunted Hollow
Havelock: S.A. Long Plantation
Hillsbourgh
  Haw Place
  Seven Hearths
Knotts Island
Lincoln County: Engleside Mansion
McAdenville: Adam Springs House
Raleigh
  Governor's Mansion
  Holman House
  Poole's Woods
Roanoke Island
Rockford: Burris House

Rutherfordton: Jailhouse
Salola Mountain
Siver City: Harper Cross Roads
Thomasville: San-Mor Inc. Factory
Troy: Sut Creek Bridge
White Oak: Old Roberson Place
Willow Creek
Wilmington: Price-Gause House
Winston-Salem
Brothers House
Salem Tavern

North Dakota
Powers Lake
Richardton: Wild Plum School

Ohio
Belmont: Woods School
Bethlehem: Woodside Pet Cemetery
Blendon: 3670 Karikal Drive
Blue Ash: Hazelwood
Bowling Green: University Apartments
Cincinnati
1020 West 8th Street
Cleveland
1115 Leading Avenue
4207 Mason Court SE
Franklin Castle
Dayton: 354 Forrest Avenue
Fayette County: Cherry Hill
Findlay: Town Cemetery
Galion: 937 Harding Avenue
Gallipolis: Deluse Farmhouse
Granville: Buxton Inn
Johnson's Island
Kent: Van Campen Hall, Kent State University
Lake Hope: Hope Furnace
Pickaway County: Timmon's Bridge
Pleasant Valley
Somerset: Otterbein Cemetery

Waterloo: Columbian House

Oklahoma

Bristow: Jailhouse
Kiamichi Mountains
Oklahoma City: Biltmore Hotel
Tulsa: Berryhill
Vinita: Circle J Ranch

Oregon

Ashland: 35 S. 2nd Street
Clackamus County: Old Campbell Land Claim
Clatsop Spit
Copper: Rouge River Campground
Eugene: Bornholz House
Portland
  546 Marshall Street
  Park Avenue
The Dalles: McNutt Home

Pennsylvania

Altoona
  Baker Mansion
  Rosella Rock
Blue Mountains: Mission House
Braddock: Thomson Works
Cheltenham: East Cheltenham Free Library
Conewago Creek: Conewago Creek Bridge
Coudersport
  Black Forest
  Cherry Springs Hotel Site
Cross Fork: Gravel Lick Trail
Fairfield
  Furnace Road
  Rombin's Nest Shop
Fishing Creek
Germantown: Loudoun Mansion
Gettysburg
  Battlefield
  Lutheran Church
  Tavern

Hammersley Park
  Hotel
  Twin Sisters
Hanover: Pigeon Hills
Harrisburg: Den Baron Farm
Honesdale: Bethany Colony Mansion
Indiana: Watt's Hill
Lafayette Hill
Levittown: Bolton Mansion
Littlestown: Route 194 Bridge
Mahoning: 1161 North Liberty Street
McKeesport: 1515 Evans Avenue
McSherrystown: Conewago Roman Catholic Chapel
Millvale: Croatian Catholic Church
New Castle: Broad Mountain
Oleona: Ole Bull Castle
Philadelphia
  Bouvier Street
  Carpenter's Hall
  Chalkley Hall
  South Fifth Street
  Stockton House
  Walnut and 5th Street
Pittsburgh
  Broad Street Tabernacle Church
  1129 Ridge Avenue
  Hawthorne Street
  KDKA-TV Station
  Lincoln Avenue
  Montview Place
  1724 Harcor Drive
Port Allegany: Two Mile Run
Prospectville: Graeme Park
Smethport: McKean County Jail
Valley Forge State Park
York: Center Square

Rhode Island
Barrington: Baron Farm
Block Island

Foster: Ramtail Factory
Hopkins Hill: Witch Rock
Johnston: 40 Pocasset Street
Mount Tom
Narragansett: Wedderburn House
North Kingstown: Swamptown
Providence: Martin Road
Quonset: Route One

South Carolina
Bamberg: U.S. 301
Bush River
Camden
Court Inn
116 Mill Street
Charleston
Belvidere Mansion
Fenwick Hall
59 Church Street
Old Goose Creek Plantation
St Philip's Church
Edisto Island
Gaston: Poor Hope Plantation
Georgetown: Litchfield Plantation
Goshen Hill: Goshen Hill Road
McClellanville: Hampton
Pawley's Island
Spartanburg: Foster's Tavern

South Dakota
Deadwood
Ellsworth Air Force Base

Tennessee
Adams: Bell Caves
Bolivar: Wedding Cake House
Charleston: Coon Hunters Headquarters Building
Chickamauga: Chickamauga National Military Park
Clarksville: Oaklands
Farmington: Hollond House
Gordonsburg: Natchez Trace Parkway/Lewis Monument

- Kingston: Pastorium
- Memphis
  - Graceland Mansion
  - 9169 Tulane Road
  - Orpheum Theatre
  - Woodruff Mansion
- Mountain City: Fiddler's Rock
- Murfreesboro: Stones River Battlefield National Park
- Nashville: 1627 9th Avenue
- Shelbyville: 610 North Jefferson Street
- Shiloh: Shiloh Battlefield/Cherry Mansion
- Snow Creek: Crazy Horse Hollow
- Sparta: Milksick Mountain
- Surgoinsville: Old White Oak
- Taylor's Community: Austin Farm

Texas

- Austin
  - Governor's Mansion
  - School for the Blind
- Brazos River: Bailey Plantation
- Brownsville
  - Community Development Corporation Office
  - Olive Electric Inc. Office
- Chisholm Hollow
- Chisos Mountains
- Cisco: Old B.Y. Woodson Place
- Dallas
  - Banner Mansion
  - Dealey Plaza
  - Prairie Avenue
  - White Rock Lake
- El Paso: Trans Mountain Road/Cotton Wood Springs
- Galveston: Mott House
- Goliad: La Bahia Mission
- Henderson: Old Howard Homestead
- Houston
  - 1110 Edwards Street
  - 1425 W. Gray Street

NASA Space Center area
106 E. Alber Street
Public Library
7224 Kernel Street
LaPorte: Lafitte House
Laredo: Laredo Independent School District's Azios Building
Llano: Ranch House
San Antonio: Brooks House
San Marcos: Bridge
San Patricio: Nueces River
Sulphur Springs: Negro Hollow
Waller County: Liendo Plantation

Utah
Salt Lake City
Bailey Seed Company
Cook Home

Vermont
Albany: Old Hayden Mansion
Chittenden
Honto's Cave
Old Eddy Homestead
Mt. Glastenbury
Waterford Township: Washburn Barn

Virginia
Abington: Martha Washington Inn
Alexandria
Lee Mansion
Ramsey House
Amelia: Haw Branch Plantation
Beaverdam: Scotchtown
Belle Haven
Bowling Green: Old Mansion
Buck Hills Caves
Cedar Creek
Charles City
Shirley Plantation
Westover Mansion
Charlottesville

  Carrsgrove
  Castle Hill
  Michie Tavern
  Monticello
  The Farm
Fork Union: Careby Hall
Fredericksburg
  Chatham/Lacy House
  Fall Hill Plantation
  Federal Hill
  Kenmore
Gloucester County
  Paynton Hall
  Rosewell
Hampton: Fort Monroe
Hanover: Barksdale Theater
Linden: Pecatone
Loudoun County: Noland House
Luray: Corry House
Mathews: Old House Woods
Middletown: Belle Grove Plantation Smoke House
Norfolk
  City Park
  Norfolk Museum
  Robin Hood Apartments
Old Rag Mountain: Pheasant Hill
Petersburg: Centre Hill Mansion
Port Royal: Elmwood Plantation
Portsmouth
  Chickahominy River
  London Street and Canal Street
  949 Florida Avenue
Richmond
  Bacon's Castle/Old Lawne Creek Church Graveyard
  Ninth Street
Stafford: Aquia Church graveyard
Staunton: Dudley Place
Virginia Beach
  Chesapeake Beach Fire and Rescue Station
  Witch Duck Point

Williamsburg
Edgewood Inn
Governor's Palace
Wyth House

Washington
Bald Mountain
Grass Mountain
Ilwaco: Beard's Hollow
Seattle
Boylston Street
905 E. Pine Street
Spokane: Monaghan Hall/Gonzaga University

West Virginia
Fayette County: Mount Carbon
Flatwoods
Knob Fork
Little Sewell Mountain
Mill Creek
Monogah: Number Six Mine
Moorefield: Cole Mountain
Point Pleasant: Chief Cornstalk Public Hunting Area
Ravenswood: Movie Theater
Rich Mountain
Ripley: Ghost Ridge
Sumnersville: Peter Creek Valley
Valley Bend
Wetzel County: Rock Camp

Wisconsin
Burke Township: Ghost Hill
Delafield: Rosslynne Manse
Evansville: East Side Steak House
Fremont: Old Gottlieb Farm
Germantown: Old Buth Farm
Hale's Corners: Layton House Inn Grounds
Hudson: Coulee Road
Lake Milles: Rock Lake
Madeline: Ojibway Burial Grounds
Madison
County Jail

Noe Woods
Seminole Highway
Merrill: Scott Mansion
Merrimac: Ferry House Inn
Milwaukee
Bading House
Giddings Boardinghouse
Grand Avenue
Hobart House
Palmer's Addition
Mineral Point: Old Military Ridge Road
Mount Horeb: Knut K. Lunde Home
Oak Hill: Pumpkin Hollow
Omro: Fox River Bridge
Oneida Lake: Indian Burial Grounds
Oshkosh: Paine Art Center
Pewaukee: Octagon House
Platteville: Negro Head
Poy Sippi
Prescott: Walnut Street
Ridgeway
Cemetery
Messerschmidt Hotel Grounds
Military Ridge Road
Petra Homestead
River Falls: Colonel Charles Parker Mansion
Shawano: Old Kopelkie Farm
Verona: Route 1
Waukesha: Ravensholme
West Algoma: Town Streets
Wisconsin Dells
Dell House
Elephant Rock

Wyoming
Telephone Canyon

Canada

Alberta
- Daysland
- Frog Lake

British Columbia
- Arrow Lakes
- Chilliwack: 342 Williams Street North
- Fraser River: Mile 81
- Morris Valley
- Oak Bay
- Vancouver
  - Race Rocks/Zone of Silence
  - West 11th Street
- Victoria: City Park/2668 Uplands

Labrador
- Chibongamon Lake

Manitoba
- Portage la Prairie: Indian Burial Grounds
- Winnipeg
  - McVicar Block
  - Mother Tucker's Restaurant
  - St. Andrews
  - St. John's Cathedral
- Woodridge

New Brunswick
- Fredericton: Christ Church Cathedral
- French Fort Cove
- Grand Manan
  - Big Wood Island
  - Cheney's Island
  - Kent Island
- Howe's Lake: Hangman's Hill
- Kennebecasis: Ryan's Castle
- Lincoln: Glasier Mansion

Lorneville: Ghost Rock
Mispec: Ghost Hollow
Moncton: Reinsborough Place
Newcastle: Dungarvon River
Restigouche River
Rexton: Richibucto-Rexton Road
Saint John: Hazen Castle Site
Saint John River: Paddy Hollow Camp

Newfoundland
Conche
Port-au-Coix

Northwest Territories and Yukon
Alcan Highway: Indian Battlefield
Mackenzie River: Camsell Bend
South Nahanni River Valley

Nova Scotia
Amherst
Cox Cottage
Princess and Church Street
Caledonia Mills: McDonald Homestead
Eastern Passage: Devil's Island
Halifax: Citadel Hill
Mineville
Sable Island
Springhill
White Head Island: Lighthouse
Yarmouth: Vengeance

Ontario
Algonquin Provincial Park
Belleville
Home for Orphaned Children
Ticonderoga Reserve
Black Lake
Brantford: St. Luke's Anglican Church
Brockville: Alban's Point
Cherry Valley
Etobicoke: Prince Edward Drive
Guelph: Rexdale

Hamilton: Brucedale Drive
Indian River
Kingston: Old Aykroyd Place
Lindsay: 33 Cambridge Street South
London: Colborne Street
Manitoulin Island
Milton: Harland Road
Mississauga: Cooksville
Moose River
Nipissing: Waterfalls Lodge
North London: McGhee Place
Peterborough: Bon Echo
Picton: Queen Street
Saint Catherine's: Garden City Dry Cleaners
Saint Thomas: Alma College
Scarborough: Lawrence Avenue East
Six Nations Reserve
South Bay: Mariner's Cemetery
Streetsville: Mississauga Road and Steeles Avenue
Sudbury: Highway 17
Thorah Island
Thornhill: Annswell
Toronto
  Ardmore Road
  Bagot Court
  Bay Street
  Bleeker Street
  Chisholm Avenue
  Colborne Lodge
  College Street
  Duke at Sherbourne Street
  Dundas Street
  Dunfield Street
  82 Bond Street
  Grand Opera House
  Hillholme Road
  Humber River
  Jarvis Street
  Mackenzie Hall

Old City Hall
174 Avenue Road
Queen Street West
Silverwood Avenue
Sumach Street
Sunnyside
University College
Walmer Road
Wellesley Street
Yorkville
Wallaceburg: Belledoon
Windsor: Old Crandall Home

Prince Edward Island
Charlottetown: Binstead
Holland Cove

Quebec
Acton Vale: Saint-Onge Home
Charlesbourg: Chateau Bigot
Hudson: Hudson Hotel
Ile Dupes: Church
Ile-aux-Coudres: Seal Rocks
Montreal
Hotel-Dieu
Queen Elizabeth Hotel
St. Sauvener
Sainte Famille Street
Quebec City: Notre-Dame-de-Grace
Richmond Gulf

Saskatchewan
Kindersley
Moose Mountain

Appendix III
Mystery Spots and Magnetic Hills

These sites should be approached as an entertaining field trip. They have mainly been created for tourists; do not expect anything other than amusing optical illusions, and you will have a good time. The accompanying list is arranged by state/province, nearest town/city, and the name given to the exact location.

Mystery Spots and Magnetic Hills

Canada

New Brunswick
Moncton: Magnetic Hill

Ontario
Craigleith: Gravity Hill
Darce: Magnetic Hill

United States of America

Arizona
Sedona: Red Rock Vortex

California
Salinas: Wonder Hill
Santa Cruz: Mystery Spot

Colorado
Beulah: Camp Birch

Florida
Lake Wales: Spook Hill

Hawaii
Molokai: Penguin Bank

Indiana
Mooresville: Strange Hill

Maine
Wilton: Spook Hill

Massachusetts
Leominster: Lowe Street Hill/Magnetic Hill

Michigan
Calumet: Tamarack Mines
Saint Ignace: Mystery Spot

Missouri
Winona: Odd Acres

New Mexico
Ruidoso Downs: Anomaly Site
Socorro: Anomaly Site

New York
Great Valley: Breathing Well
Olean: Country Lane
Portville: Promised Land Road

North Carolina
Bentonville: Battleground/Neuse Vortex
Boone: Mystery Hill

Ohio
Marblehead: Mystery Hill

Oregon
Cave Junction: Mini-Vortex
Gold Hill: Oregon Vortex
Shady Cove: Uncanny Canyon
Siskiyou Mountains: Vortex

Wisconsin
Lake Delton: Wonder Spot

Please note: New Hampshire's North Salem site of "Mystery Hill" is a true megalithic wonder and should not be placed in the same category as the locations in this list.

Sources

Readers interested in obtaining more information on the specific locations of curious wonders are referred to my twenty-two-page Regional Bibliography in *Mysterious America*.

For the latest Fortean news, please write:

Institute of Fortean Studies (IFS)
124 Ocean Avenue
Portland, Maine 04103

Fortean Times
96 Mansfield Road
London NW3 2HX
United Kingdom

UFO Newsclipping Service
Route 1, Box 200
Plumerville, Arkansas 72127

Vestigia
56 Brookwood Road
Stanhope, New Jersey 07874

The Society for the Investigation of the Unexplained
Box 265
Little Silver, New Jersey 07739

International Fortean Organization
Box 367
Arlington, Virginia 22210

International Society of Cryptozoology
Box 43070
Tucson, Arizona 85733

or I would be happy to exchange information with any of my readers:

Loren Coleman
P.O. Box 109
Rangeley, Maine 04970.

Index by States and Provinces (Refer also to individual state/province listings under each appendix.)